A Guide to
SPACE

Kevin Pettman

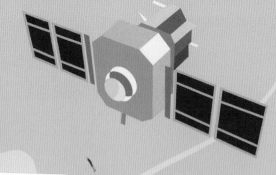

Published in paperback in 2020 by Wayland
Copyright © Hodder and Stoughton, 2019

Written by Kevin Pettman
Design by Simon Letchford
Edited by Catherine Brereton

ISBN: 978 1 5263 0738 5

Wayland, an imprint of
Hachette Children's Group
Part of Hodder and Stoughton
Carmelite House
50 Victoria Embankment
London EC4Y 0DZ

An Hachette UK Company
www.hachette.co.uk
www.hachettechildrens.co.uk

Printed in China
10 9 8 7 6 5 4 3 2 1

Picture acknowledgements (cover and inside pages): All images and graphic elements used are courtesy of Shutterstock. Every attempt has been made to clear copyright. Should there be any inadvertent omission, please apply to the Publisher for rectification.

The website addresses (URLs) listed in this book were valid at the time of going to press. However, it is possible that the contents or addresses may have changed since the publication of this book. No responsibility for any such changes can be accepted by either the author or the Publisher.

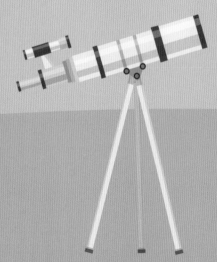

Contents

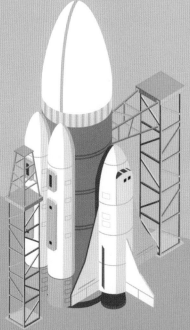

See into space

Welcome to space! Here you can gaze into our solar system and see how the Sun, the eight planets and other space objects match up. It's an amazing, fact-packed world out there ...

The **Sun** is nearly 1.4 million kilometres wide, is 330,000 times heavier than Earth and has a surface temperature over 5,500°C (see pages 10–11).

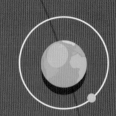

Earth is the third planet from the Sun and the biggest of the four rocky inner planets. It has the right combination of water, oxygen, sunlight and temperatures to support life (see pages 16–17).

Jupiter weighs more than double all the other planets combined, and 1,321 Earths could fit inside it. Moving outwards from the Sun, it's the first of the four gas giants (see pages 24–25).

The only other object in the universe that humans have stood on, Earth's **Moon** is an average of 384,400 kilometres away from us and is the brightest object in the night sky (see pages 18–19).

Mercury is the smallest planet in our solar system but also the fastest traveller. It speeds through its orbit at 170,503 kilometres an hour (see pages 12–13).

With ice and a type of salty liquid water around the surface, scientists continue to study **Mars** for signs of life. The Opportunity space rover has been exploring its surface since 2004 (see pages 20–21).

The **Asteroid Belt**, between Mars and Jupiter, is home to hundreds of millions of space rocks. It is an estimated 225 million kilometres wide (see pages 22–23).

Venus is the hottest planet at between 462°C and 470°C. Its scorching temperatures and poisonous gases mean humans could never survive on it (see pages 14–15).

The first man in space was **Yuri Gagarin** in 1961. **Valentina Tereshkova** was the first woman in space in 1963 (see pages 46–47).

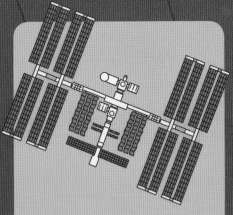

The **International Space Station** took 13 years to build, and travels around the Earth 16 times a day. Up to six astronauts can live on the ISS at a time (see pages 48–49).

Stars look small from Earth, but many are actually bigger than our star, the Sun. There are billions of stars in the universe (see pages 38–39).

With temperatures below -200°C, **Uranus** is a cold and distant planet. Parts of it can experience 21 years of continual darkness (see pages 32–33).

Discovered in 1930, **Pluto** is the biggest of the dwarf planets that exist beyond Neptune. Pluto orbits the Sun in a zone called the Kuiper Belt (see pages 36–37).

With seven main rings running around it, **Saturn** is one of the most easily recognised planets. It also has 53 confirmed moons (see pages 30–31).

Neptune is the furthest planet from the Sun and takes an incredible 165 Earth years to orbit the Sun (see pages 34–35).

Understanding space words

Space may seem complex and mind boggling, but if you can understand these key words and phrases it will help you get a clearer picture of what's going on above Earth.

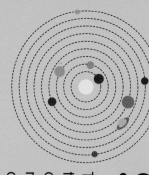

Solar system

The solar system is made up of a star and the objects that travel around it. These objects can be planets, asteroids, moons, meteoroids and comets. The star at the centre of our solar system is the Sun.

Space

Space starts at about 100 kilometres above Earth. It has no breathable air. It looks black because there aren't enough oxygen molecules to make it look blue.

Universe

Everything that exists, including stars, planets and everything on and around them, and everything that will develop in the future, are part of the universe.

Atom

An atom is the smallest particle of a chemical element. Atoms join together to form molecules. Atoms are made up of protons, electrons and neutrons.

Planet

A planet is an object that orbits around the Sun, has a nearly round shape and has a clear path in which it moves around the Sun. Dwarf planets, like Pluto, are different because they usually have other objects crossing their path.

Big Bang

The Big Bang is what most experts think was the start of the universe. About 13.8 billion years ago, something incredibly tiny exploded and expanded rapidly to begin forming the universe. After about 4.6 billion years the Sun was formed, followed by the planets.

Galaxy

Our solar system is part of the Milky Way galaxy. A galaxy is a massive collection of gas, dust and billions of stars.

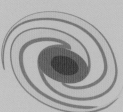

Star

A star is a big ball of gas with tremendous light and heat. Stars are formed when clouds of gas and dust collapse and break up.

Astronomer

An astronomer is a scientist who studies objects in the sky. Famous astronomers of the past include Nicolaus Copernicus, Johannes Kepler, Galileo Galilei, Sir Isaac Newton and Claudius Ptolemy.

Mass

The mass of something, like a planet or star, means how much stuff it is made of. It is not the same as weight, which is a force acting on that stuff.

Speed of light

Light travels at a speed of 299,792,458 metres per second.

Matter

Objects that have mass and take up space are called matter. Planets, moons, gases and even humans are made up of matter!

Astronomical unit

One astronomical unit (AU) is equal to 149,597,870,700 metres (roughly 150 billion metres). It is the approximate distance between the Earth and Sun and is a useful measuring distance in space science.

1AU

Atmosphere

The atmosphere is made up of the gases surrounding a planet, such as Earth, as well as other objects like stars and some moons.

Satellite

An object in an orbit is a satellite. This can be a natural object, such as a moon, or a human-made object like the International Space Station or a space telescope.

Astronaut

A person who travels in a spacecraft into space.

Orbit

An orbit is a regular and repeated path that one object takes around another in space.

Light year

A light year is the distance light can travel in one year (365 days). It is equal to about 9.5 trillion kilometres.

NASA

The National Aeronautics and Space Administration (NASA) is an American government agency that looks after space travel, exploration and research.

How the universe began

The formation of the universe was incredibly complex and took thousands of millions of years. Here you can see how it all happened, starting with a rather big event nearly 14 billion years ago.

Scientists think the universe began to form about 13.8 billion years ago, in something called the **Big Bang**. Space did not exist before this.

Within **the first few minutes** the universe's temperature was a still-unbelievable 1 billion degrees Celsius. It's often described by scientists as being like a dark, giant boiling soup of super-hot particles.

Next **the universe began to cool** and particles of energy became the beginnings of atoms and the basis of future planets, stars, galaxies … everything that has ever existed!

In a tiny fraction of a second, something hundreds of times smaller than a pinhead exploded in a **huge eruption** and expanded to become the universe.

1 2 3 4 5 6

The universe expanded rapidly in size in a millionth of a second – a period of time called the **Inflation Era**.

The **temperature** at the time of this unimaginable explosion was billions of degrees Celsius.

After 300,000 years the first **atoms of hydrogen and helium** formed. The universe's temperature was around 3,000°C.

At this time light appeared too. Light energy called photons could pass through the cleared, empty space.

The **first stars** appeared 200 million years after the Big Bang. Stars are created when clouds of dust and gas collapse inwards.

The Sun, which is the nearest star to Earth, was formed about 4.5 billion years ago from space dust and gases.

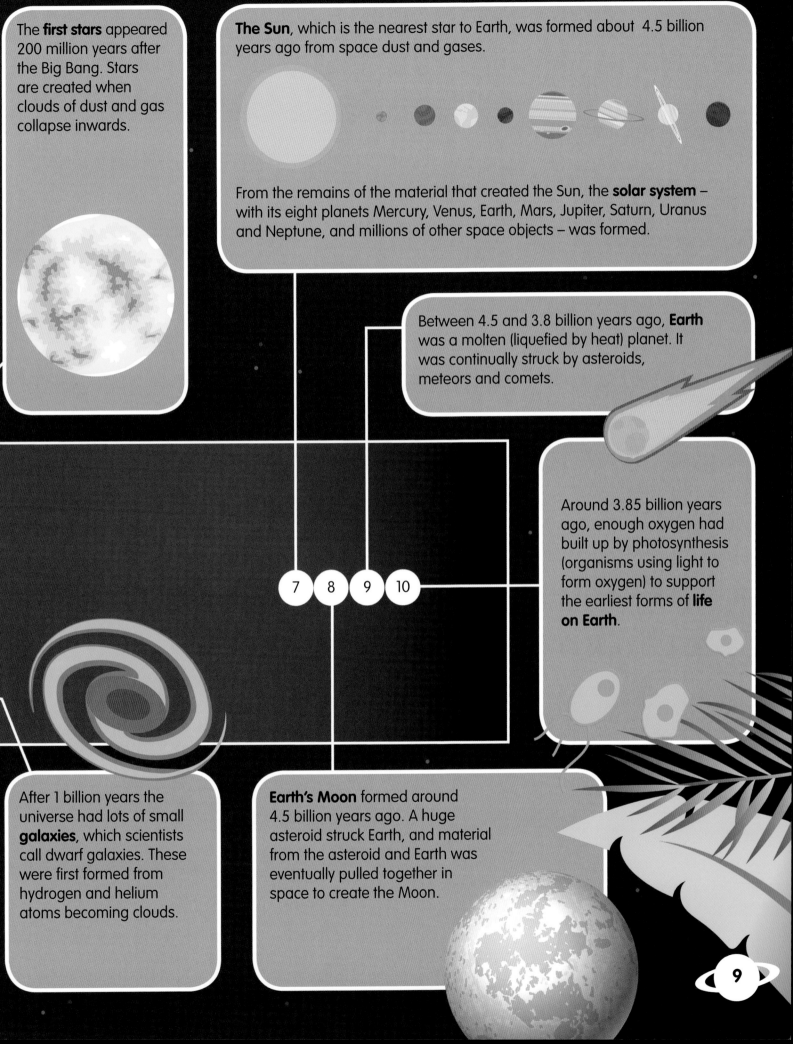

From the remains of the material that created the Sun, the **solar system** – with its eight planets Mercury, Venus, Earth, Mars, Jupiter, Saturn, Uranus and Neptune, and millions of other space objects – was formed.

Between 4.5 and 3.8 billion years ago, **Earth** was a molten (liquefied by heat) planet. It was continually struck by asteroids, meteors and comets.

Around 3.85 billion years ago, enough oxygen had built up by photosynthesis (organisms using light to form oxygen) to support the earliest forms of **life on Earth**.

7 8 9 10

After 1 billion years the universe had lots of small **galaxies**, which scientists call dwarf galaxies. These were first formed from hydrogen and helium atoms becoming clouds.

Earth's Moon formed around 4.5 billion years ago. A huge asteroid struck Earth, and material from the asteroid and Earth was eventually pulled together in space to create the Moon.

The Sun: hot facts and figures

The Sun is Earth's closest star, but it's still nearly 150 million kilometres from Earth. Without its powerful energy and heat, life would not exist on our planet – so here are a stack of important facts about the solar system's most important object.

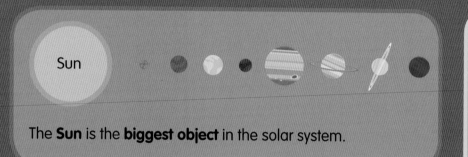

Sun

The **Sun** is the **biggest object** in the solar system.

Burrrrrp!

More than 1 million Earths could fit inside the Sun.

All the solar system's other planets could too, hundreds of times.

The diameter of the Sun is 1,392,684 km.

The Sun is 330,000 times heavier than Earth.

x 330,000

The Sun is a giant ball of glowing gas. 91 per cent of its atoms are **hydrogen** and 8.9 per cent are **helium**.

8.9% helium   0.1% other

91% hydrogen

Tiny traces of at least 67 other elements are also there, including oxygen, carbon, nitrogen and iron.

Every 11 years the **Sun's layers** go through changes and can become violent, causing space weather and damage to human structures such as satellites and power grids.

8 minutes 20 seconds

The time it takes photosphere radiation (**sunlight**) to reach Earth after it leaves the Sun, travelling at a speed of about 300,000 kilometres per second.

Scientists think the **Sun will burn for between 10 to 11 billion years,** which means it has around 6 billion years of life left.

It burns through 600,000,000,000 kg of fuel per second.

Solar wind carries the Sun's magnetic field outwards from the star, in all directions. These can reach Earth and cause night-time light displays called auroras.

The **surface of the Sun** is incredibly hot, at over 5,500°C. The hottest temperature ever reached on Earth is 57.8°C.

The core (centre) of the Sun is an unbelievable 15 million °C.

The Sun's surface is hot enough to boil diamond, one of the toughest materials on Earth.

6 regions, or layers, make up the Sun ...

Core is where nuclear reactions between hydrogen atoms make helium.

Convective zone carries energy to the surface, which takes 170,000 years to reach the surface.

Chromosphere is the thin layer of atmosphere next to the Sun.

10%
The Sun's luminosity (brightness) increases by 10 per cent every 1 billion years.

Radiative zone sees energy spread outwards.

Photosphere is the bright visible surface, but it's a 500 km-thick gas layer, not a solid surface.

Corona is the outer atmosphere, where sunspots and solar flares can happen.

2
The minimum number of **solar eclipses** which can be seen from Earth each year, although these can be partial eclipses. A solar eclipse happens when the Moon passes in front of the Sun and covers it from view.

WARNING!

Never look directly at the Sun, even through sunglasses or a telescope. It can seriously damage your eyes.

When the **Sun begins to die,** it will probably expand and engulf Mercury, Venus and Earth before collapsing in on itself.

RIP
SUN

RIP
MERCURY

RIP
VENUS

RIP
EARTH

Birds often go quiet during an eclipse because they think it's night.

A meeting with Mercury

Small and speedy is a good description of the rocky planet Mercury. From extreme temperatures to huge craters and maybe even some ice caps, there's lots going on under its very thin atmosphere.

Mercury is the **closest planet to the Sun**, between 47 million and 70 million kilometres away.

Long days …

A day on Mercury takes 59 Earth days. This is the time it takes for Mercury to spin once.

It takes just 88 days for Mercury to orbit the Sun and it's the fastest planet. It speeds through space at 170,503 kilometres per hour.

That's over **450** times faster than a Formula 1 car's top speed.

Mercury is **4,879 kilometres wide** – less than half the width of Earth. Mercury is the **smallest planet** in our solar system – only a little bigger than Earth's Moon.

Mercury looks like Earth's Moon, with **craters formed by meteorites** crashing into its surface more than 3.5 billion years ago.

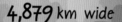

4,879 km wide

Fast-travelling Mercury is named after the super-fast Roman god of trade, travellers and messengers.

Mercury is the **darkest planet** because it reflects only 11 per cent of the sunlight it gets.

Experts also think Mercury is so dark because carbon underneath its outer crust gives it a very dark appearance.

610°C

That's the temperature range on Mercury – more than on any other planet. During the day it can be 430°C but it can drop to an incredibly cold -180°C at night.

-180°C   0°C   430°C

At times the Sun appears **3** times bigger when seen from Mercury than it does from Earth.

Mercury is so sunny that NASA's **Messenger spacecraft** had a special sunshade when it explored the planet from orbit.

So if someone weighs 100 kg on Earth they would only weigh 38 kg on Mercury.

The surface gravity on Mercury is only about 38 per cent of what it is on Earth.

sunshade

250 km
1,550 km

A crater wider than 250 kilometres is called a basin. Mercury's Caloris Basin is the largest at 1,550 kilometres.

Launched in 2004, by 2013 Messenger had mapped every square metre of Mercury's surface.

Experts think there may be **ice** in deep craters at the north and south poles of Mercury, where the land is in permanent shadow.

Because it's in between the Sun and Earth, very occasionally Mercury can be seen from Earth passing across the face of the Sun. This is called a **transit** and happens 13 times a century.

11 November 2019
13 November 2032
The dates of the next two transits.

Mercury has been divided into regions, which include valleys, plains, craters and steep slopes. Many are named after famous people.

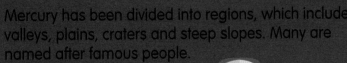

Tolstoy Basin (Russian writer Leo Tolstoy)

Beethoven Region (German composer Ludwig van Beethoven)

Shakespeare Region (English poet and playwright William Shakespeare)

Venus: a beauty and a beast

Venus appears as a bright and beautiful planet when seen from Earth, but beneath its clouds it's a frightening place of baking heat and lethal gases. Take a close-up look if you dare …

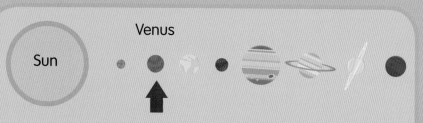
Venus

Sun

Venus is the **closest planet to us**, and the second from the Sun, but it still only comes within 40 million kilometres of Earth.

Atmosphere

96.5% carbon dioxide

3.5% nitrogen and other trace gases

Venus is sometimes called **Earth's 'evil twin'**. It's only slightly smaller than our planet, at 12,104 kilometres in diameter, and has similar rocks. But it would be a deadly place for humans because of …

There is only a few degrees temperature difference between its poles and equator.

poisonous gases

scorching temperatures

crushing atmosphere

After the Sun and our Moon, Venus is the **brightest natural object** in the sky. Its dense clouds reflect sunlight back into space to give it its famous glow.

It's the hottest planet in our solar system – almost always between 462°C and 470°C.

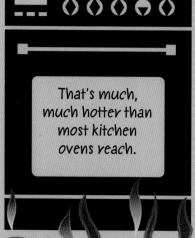
That's much, much hotter than most kitchen ovens reach.

500°C

The **greenhouse effect**, where carbon dioxide in the atmosphere stops heat escaping into space, raises the temperature on Venus by a huge 500°C. On Earth the figure is about 35°C.

Its beautiful appearance is the reason it was named Venus, after the Roman goddess of beauty.

The hottest spots on Earth only reach around 50°C.

Venus spins on its axis the opposite way to Earth, meaning the Sun rises in the west and sets in the east.

Venus is only **tilted on its axis by 3 degrees**, whereas Earth is about 23 degrees. This means Venus doesn't have seasons and is very hot all the time.

There are two main **high regions** on Venus, which are called uplands.

Aphrodite Terra is about the size of Africa.

Ishtar Terra is the size of Australia.

If you could stand on Venus, the **surface pressure** of the atmosphere's gases on you would be 90 times heavier than it is on Earth.

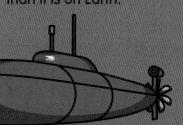

That's the same pressure a submarine feels 900 m below water.

900 m

Clouds lie between 50 km and 70 km above the surface.

The constant clouds are toxic and full of sulphuric acid droplets.

The first spacecraft to land on Venus was the USSR's probe Venera 7 in 1970.

CCCP

In December 2015, Japan's Akatsuki spacecraft entered into the orbit of Venus.

Even though it shines brightly, Venus's **rocky surface** isn't visible from Earth because of its heavy clouds.

Venus's craters are large, up to 300 kilometres wide, because only big meteorites can get through its atmosphere and smash into the surface.

1,600+
Venus has **more known volcanoes** than any other planet.

Venus's surface is covered by:

☑ mountains ☑ volcanoes

☑ craters ☑ huge lava plains

Radar images have made scientists think there may be **recent lava flows** on Venus and that some of its volcanoes are still active.

What on Earth?

Earth is unique and supports life like no other known planet. Its abundant water and oxygen, plus relatively stable temperatures and weather, are vital for life on Earth to survive.

Earth

Sun

Earth is the **third planet from the Sun** and the biggest of the four inner planets, known as the rocky planets, which are Mercury, Venus, Earth and Mars.

Earth

7.5 billion humans

391,000 plant species

7,770,000 animal species

149,600,00 km from the Sun

12,746 km
wide

Plants on Earth create oxygen by using sunlight, in a process called photosynthesis.

Animals and plants use oxygen to respire (breathe) and to provide their energy.

Earth:
the one and only

☑ Only planet known to have lots of liquid water

☑ Only planet to have life (that we know of)

☑ Warm, but not so hot that humans boil

☑ Only known atmosphere where humans can breathe

More than 70 per cent of Earth's surface is covered by **oceans**. The largest is the Pacific Ocean, which is about 165 million square km and covers around 32 per cent of Earth.

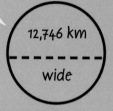

-92°C   15°C   56.7°C

Earth's **average temperature** is around 15°C. The highest recorded temperature is 56.7°C and the lowest is -92°C.

Earth has been called the **'Goldilocks' planet** because everything is just right for life to exist.

Goldilocks in the children's story chose everything that was 'just right': porridge that was not too hot or too cold, a chair that was not too big or too small, a bed that was not too hard or too soft.

Crust

Split into massive plates that float on the mantle. Earthquakes happen and deep trenches are formed when the plates collide.

Mantle

Nearly 3,000 km deep and made with silicate rocks packed with magnesium and iron. When **rocks** in the mantle get hot and rise, then cool and sink to the core, it causes the Earth's plates to move.

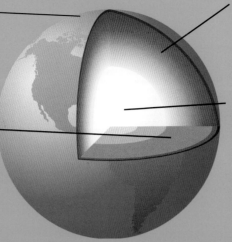

Outer core

Liquid, made mainly of molten iron and around 2,260 km thick. Temperature is over 4,400°C.

Inner core

Heavy, made mainly of iron and around 2,440 km in diameter. Temperature is over 6,000°C but it stays solid because of the enormous pressure on it.

It takes Earth **365** days to orbit the Sun.

24 hours
The time it takes Earth to spin completely on its axis.

23.44 degrees
How far the Earth is tilted in relation to the Sun.

Parts of the Earth tilted towards the Sun = long bright days and warm weather (summer)

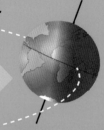

107,200 km/h The average speed that the Earth orbits the Sun.

Parts tilted away from the Sun = colder weather and shorter days (winter)

78% nitrogen
21% oxygen
1% other, including carbon dioxide, argon and water vapour

Earth's atmosphere

6 layers in Earth's atmosphere ...

6. Exosphere – Earth's outer layer extends to around 10,000 km above Earth and is full of hydrogen and helium. Many satellites orbit Earth here.

5. Ionosphere – gases here make electrical charges. This layer overlaps part of the thermosphere, mesosphere and exosphere and ranges from 80 km to 600 km above Earth's surface.

4. Thermosphere – temperatures reach 2,400°C. This layer is about 513 km thick. Home to the ISS and low Earth orbit satellites.

3. Mesosphere – extending to about 85 km high, this cold layer experiences temperatures of about -100°C. This is where meteors burn up in Earth's atmosphere.

2. Stratosphere – the second layer from Earth's surface extends to about 50 km high. It contains the ozone layer that protects Earth from the Sun's radiation.

1. Troposphere – this layer extends from about 8 km to 14.5 km above Earth's surface. Mostly made of nitrogen and oxygen and contains most of Earth's weather.

Over the Moon

Outside of Earth, the Moon is the only place where humans have walked. It may appear dark and dismal but on its dusty surface, and deep below, there's much to explore.

The Earth's **Moon** is thought to be **around 4.5 billion years old**. It got its cratered surface during the first 750 million years of its life, when it was struck by asteroids and comets.

Moon

Earth

Volcanic lava squeezed through the cracks and filled the biggest craters.

The Moon is on average **384,400 kilometres away from Earth**. It can be between 363,100 and 406,700 kilometres away.

Diameter of 3,476 km, which is less than one third the diameter of Earth.

123°C — The maximum temperature of the Moon's surface when in full daylight.

0°C —

The minimum temperature on the Moon when it's in darkness.

−233°C —

Earth's Moon is the **5th largest moon** in the solar system.

 Ganymede

 Callisto

 Europa

 Io

 Earth's Moon

The largest 'dark spot' (crater) on the Moon is the **Oceanus Procellarum**, covering about 4 million square kilometres.

Earth's oceans and seas:

High tide on Earth is caused by the Moon's gravity forcing water to bulge out on the side of the Earth closest to the Moon.

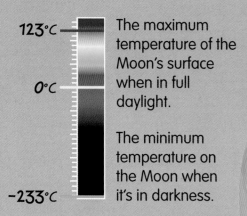

Low tide is when the side of Earth furthest from the Moon has less gravity pulling on oceans and seas.

The Moon's highest point is 1,938 metres higher than Mount Everest.

10,786 metres

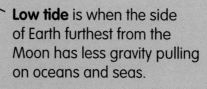

Earth ➡

30 Earths could fit in a line between Earth and the Moon.

The Moon is made up of ...

Crust
Between 70 km and 150 km thick and made of oxygen, silicon, magnesium, iron, calcium and aluminium with traces of titanium, uranium, thorium, potassium and hydrogen.

Mantle
Could be up to 1,000 km thick and probably made of minerals like magnesium, iron, silicon and oxygen.

Core
Solid, iron-rich inner core 480 km thick covered by a liquid iron shell 90 km thick and a molten layer 150 km thick.

1959

The year the Soviet Union's Luna 3 space probe first photographed the side of the Moon that can't be seen from Earth.

The surface is covered in smashed rock and dust called regolith.

The Moon's appearance:
- ☑ Desert-like
- ☑ Mountains
- ☑ Valleys
- ☑ Plains
- ☑ Black sky

59%

The amount of the Moon's surface that's **visible from Earth**. The Moon orbits Earth once every 28 days and spins once in this time. This means the same side of the Moon always faces Earth.

Both sides of the Moon have two weeks of darkness, then two weeks of sunlight.

The 'other' side of the Moon is often called the 'dark side'.

382 kg

The US space agency NASA brought 382 kg of the **Moon's rock**, pebbles, sand and dust back to Earth to study.

That's about the weight of five adult men.

Gravity on the Moon is much weaker than on Earth. On the Moon, humans only weigh about one sixth of what they weigh on Earth. This means humans can jump about six times higher on the Moon.

Wheeeeee!

 ← Moon

×12

Between 1969 and 1972, **12 men walked on the Moon's** surface.

Get red-y to meet Mars

Mars is very distinctive with its bright red appearance. It's the planet humans have spent most time exploring and studying, with ice caps and salty ice suggesting life may once have existed there.

Mars

Sun

Mars, the fourth planet from the Sun, is often called the **red planet**. It looks red because of soil on its surface, which contains iron oxide – which is like rust. The air can sometimes be orangey-red when gigantic dust storms cover Mars. Mars also has the largest dust storms in the solar system.

Mars's atmosphere is made of…

- 95.3% carbon dioxide
- 2.7% nitrogen
- 1.6% argon
- 0.2% oxygen, carbon dioxide and other gases

Very thin and unbreathable atmosphere

228 million km from the Sun

6,792 km wide

Mars is 6,792 kilometres wide, which is slightly more than half Earth's size.

Mars is the second smallest planet in our solar system.

In 2015 it was *discovered* that there is salty water on the surface of Mars.

Average temperature **-63°C**

The **temperature on Mars** depends on where on the planet the temperature is measured and the season.

Temperature range -120°C to 30°C

Mars has large amounts of ice at its North and South poles.

Scientists have calculated the ice caps are 3 kilometres thick on average. If melted, the ice would cover the surface in 5.6 metres of water.

The **distance between Earth and Mars** varies significantly, depending on where both objects are in orbit.

54.6 million km – minimum distance

401 million km – maximum distance

225 million km – average distance

NASA scientists think around 60 **meteorites** discovered on Earth came from Mars – blasted off Mars by meteoroid impacts.

August 2003

Mars was closer to Earth than at any time in the last 60,000 years. It was 55,758,006 kilometres away.

It was the closest the planets will be until August 2287.

Phobos and Deimos

These are the two small potato-shaped **moons of Mars**. Phobos is larger, at 27 kilometres at its widest point, and orbits Mars every 7.5 hours.

Mars doesn't have a ring, but experts think it will have in future. Phobos will be destroyed by Mars's gravity and may create a ring – probably in about 10 to 50 million years time.

Mars experiences winter and summer seasons, a little like Earth does. The winter is much colder and summer more mild.

Mars tilts 25 degrees on its axis (Earth tilts 23.5 degrees).

25°

Since the 1970s, space scientists have been sending spacecraft to study Mars.

Mars is home to the largest volcano in the solar system. **Olympus Mons** is over 26 kilometres tall and 700 kilometres across.

× 68

That's 68 times taller than the Empire State Building in New York, USA.

4,000 km – The length of the **Valles Marineris**, which is the longest canyon known in the solar system:

As deep as 8 km in places

Stretches nearly 20% of the distance around Mars

Probably a crack formed as the planet cooled.

1976
Viking 1 became the first craft to successfully land on Mars.

2004
NASA's Opportunity rover landed on Mars and is still travelling and exploring.

45 km+
The distance Opportunity has covered on Mars.

4,000 km

Belting around in orbit

Between the four rocky inner planets and four gas giants lies an interesting band of rocks. There are millions, probably billions, of relatively small objects in this vast region called the Asteroid Belt. There are a few big ones to watch out for too!

About 90 per cent of our solar system's asteroids can be found orbiting the Sun in the main **Asteroid Belt**, between Mars and Jupiter.

Vesta is the largest asteroid in the belt at about 530 kilometres in diameter. The smallest asteroids are less than 10 metres in diameter.

Between 1.1 to 1.9 million asteroids larger than 1 kilometre in diameter are thought to be in the Asteroid Belt.

There are millions and millions of much smaller asteroids.

NASA describes asteroids as **ancient space rubble** left over after the solar system formed more than 4 billion years ago.

225 million km
The estimated width of the Asteroid Belt.

Ceres is 950 kilometres wide and was once called an asteroid. In 2006 it was re-classified as a dwarf planet because it's so big.

Asteroids in the belt usually stay between 1 and 3 million kilometres apart.

3 million kilometres

1 million kilometres

8 asteroids are larger than 300 kilometres wide and these are spherical. Most are small and elongated though, and can look like giant peanuts!

Over 170 **craters on Earth** show where asteroids have crashed into its surface. One crater, in the Gulf of Mexico, was formed 65 million years ago and the impact is thought to have led to the **extinction of dinosaurs**.

Trojans are asteroids outside of the Asteroid Belt that share a planet's orbit but don't collide with it. Jupiter has millions of trojan asteroids.

Mars, Neptune and Earth also have trojans.

150+

The number of asteroids known to have a small moon orbiting them. Some have two moons.

Over 15,000 asteroids have been officially named. Some have unusual names …

Mr Spock

Freddiemercury

Tolkien

James Bond

Tomhanks and Megryan

Petit-Prince

Asteroids are put into 3 types:

C – 'Chondrite' asteroids are the most common, made up of mainly clay and silicate rocks.

S – 'Stony' asteroids are made of silicate and nickel-iron.

M – 'Metallic' asteroids consist of nickel-iron.

Over **100 meteorites** are thought to hit Earth every year, but most of them are very small.

A meteorite is a small piece of space rock (much smaller than an asteroid) that gets through Earth's atmosphere and reaches Earth's surface.

Asteroids that enter Earth's orbital path are called **Earth crossers**. Over 15,000 Earth crossers are known.

Asteroids that come within about 45 million km of Earth are called near-Earth asteroids.

54,000 kg

… is the weight of the largest meteorite found on Earth, in Namibia in Africa. It's called the Hoba.

… thats 24 times the weight of a white rhino.

Jupiter the giant

The biggest of the four outer planets, known as gas giants, Jupiter is truly colossal. More than 1,000 times bigger than Earth, this heavyweight packs a big punch in the universe.

Sun   Jupiter

Jupiter is the **fifth planet** from the Sun. It took most of the mass left over in the solar system after the Sun was formed 4.5 billion years ago.

Jupiter spins on its axis faster than any other planet in our solar system. It completes a rotation in less than **10** Earth hours.

Ganymede

The average temperature in the clouds of Jupiter is about **-145°C**

×2

It weighs more than twice all the other planets put together.

A year on Jupiter lasts for **4,333** Earth days.

With a diameter of 143,000 km, 11 Earths could fit side by side along it.

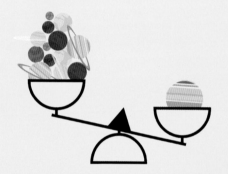

On average Jupiter is 778 million km from the Sun.

Callisto

The number of Earths that could fit inside Jupiter:

Earth → **1,321**

Jupiter

Jupiter has **69** possible **moons**. **53** are confirmed, and the **4** biggest are called the Galilean moons.

They are: Ganymede, Callisto, Europa and Io.

Ganymede is the largest moon in the solar system at 5,262 km wide.

Europa

Jupiter has a **cloudy atmosphere** that's 1,000 km thick.

10.2% helium

89.8% hydrogen

Beneath the atmosphere Jupiter has no solid surface, so spacecraft would never be able to land there.

Spacecraft can't fly through its atmosphere because the pressure would crush them.

Jupiter has the **strongest magnetic field in the solar system** because of powerful liquid metallic hydrogen under its clouds.

On the cloud tops, Jupiter's magnetic field is **20 times** stronger than on Earth.

Jupiter's atmosphere (the bit we can see) looks like colourful, swirling bands of clouds. The bands make the planet look stripy.

The dark bands are called **belts**. **=** gas falling

The brighter bands are known as **zones.** **=** gas rising from warm interior and condensing into clouds

Inside Jupiter, at its core, the **temperature** may rage to 24,000°C. Some experts even predict it's as hot as

50,000°C!

24.8 m/s^2

9.8 m/s^2

The force of **gravity in Jupiter's atmosphere** is 2.5 times stronger than on Earth.

100 kg

250 kg

of Jupiter. The **Great Red Spot** is a fierce and distinctive storm towards the south

Io

An object weighing 100 kilograms on Earth would be 250 kilograms on Jupiter.

That's really heavy, man!

Storm has raged for over **300** years

Winds inside the storm reach **539** km/h

2 times the size of Earth

More marvellous moons

There are hundreds of moons travelling around our solar system, many with strange and spectacular features just as amazing as the planets they orbit.

The two **moons of Mars, Phobos and Deimos**, are some of the smallest in the solar system.

Phobos orbits only 6,000 kilometres above Mars and is the closest known moon to its planet.

It moves 1.8 metres nearer to Mars every 100 years. In about 10 to 50 million years it will hit Mars or break up and create a ring.

Mercury is the closest planet to the Sun. The Sun's gravity would probably make any moon crash into Mercury or even into the Sun itself.

The Earthlings won't suspect a thing!

Mercury – 0 moons

Venus – 0 moons

Moon

Earth – 1 moon

Deimos

Phobos

Mars – 2 moons

Two of Saturn's inner moons, Atlas and Pan, have a ridge that gives them a distinctive 'flying saucer' shape.

Callisto   Europa

Ganymede   Io

Jupiter – 60+ moons

Saturn's biggest moon is **Titan**. Titan is larger than Earth's Moon.

It's the only moon in the solar system with a thick atmosphere. The atmosphere's pressure is 60 per cent greater than Earth's – about the same pressure as at the bottom of a swimming pool.

Rhea   Tethys

Titan   Iapetus

Saturn – 50+ moons

Titania   Umbriel   Miranda

Oberon   Ariel   Puck

Uranus – 27 moons

Titan's atmosphere extends 10 times higher than Earth's, to about 600 kilometres into space.

Plastic moon?

In 2013 **propylene** was found in Titan's atmosphere. Propylene is an ingredient used to make plastic.

Triton   Nereid

Proteus

Neptune – 13 moons

0

Experts are not sure why Venus has no moon.

The number of moons that Mercury and Venus have.

Of Jupiter's 53 known moons, **Ganymede** is the largest. It is also the biggest satellite (moon) we know of.

5,262 km diameter

Larger than Mercury and Pluto

Icy surface may contain rock

Ganymede may have a very thin **oxygen atmosphere**, but not enough to sustain life as we know it.

One of Uranus's most fascinating moons is called **Miranda**.

500 km wide

10 minutes

The time a rock would take to hit the bottom if dropped from Miranda's highest cliff.

Miranda was discovered by Gerard P. Kuiper in 1948.

One way ticket to Triton, please.

Neptune's largest moon, **Triton**, is one of the coldest places in the solar system and its surface temperature can drop to -235°C.

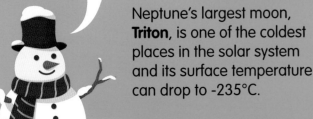

By Jupiter!

Io, the third largest of Jupiter's moons, is the most volcanic place in the solar system.

Large moons of neighbouring Europa and Ganymede help create massive tides on Io's surface.

Volcanic plumes shoot 300 km above the ground.

400,000 volts of power form lightning in Io's upper atmosphere.

X 20

Charon, the largest of Pluto's five known moons, is 20 times closer to Pluto than the Moon is to Earth.

Charon is nearly half the size of Pluto and the two are in a 'double planet system', which is unique in our solar system.

Volcanic Io

Comets close-up

Millions of kilometres away and often not visible for decades at a time, comets are tricky space features to see. Take a close-up look here and spot some spectacular comet facts.

Comets are made from **ice, rocks, gas and dust** left over when planets formed billions of years ago. Like planets, comets orbit the Sun.

When comets get closer to the Sun, the Sun's heat turns the gas into a **tail** and the dust into another long tail that can stream for millions of kilometres. When sunlight reflects off them, the tails are usually bright enough to be seen from Earth.

5,253

The number of known comets in our solar system.

Comets that come towards the inner solar system originate from the Kuiper Belt (see page 5), a region beyond Neptune. These comets can orbit the Sun in under 200 years and are called **short-period comets**.

The **centre of a comet** is called the nucleus. It is solid, dark and usually only about 1 kilometre wide. The bright, heated cloud of gases around the nucleus is known as a coma.

coma   tail

The largest known nucleus is 40 km wide.

Comet Hyakutake had a tail about 580 million kilometres long, which is the longest tail ever observed and more than four times the distance from the Earth to the Sun.

100 billion +

The possible number of comets in the Oort Cloud.

The Oort Cloud is between 5,000 and 100,000 astronomical units (AU) from the Sun.

Most comets orbit in a distant ring of debris, beyond Pluto, called the **Oort Cloud**. Some take millions of years to travel once around the Sun.

MON

TUE
17-21 °C

WED
+ 16-20 °C

The word comet comes from the Greek word 'kometes', which means long hair and refers to a comet's tail.

I told you it'd come round again!

Meteors, also called shooting stars, are tiny pieces of comet dust that burn in the atmosphere about 100 kilometres high. Meteors are a common sight from Earth – when Earth passes through a comet's dust trail it creates a meteor shower.

January, August and November are usually good times to observe meteor showers.

When to see famous meteor showers:
Quadrantids – December/January
Lyrids – April
Perseids – August
Orionids – October
Leonids – November
Geminids – December

Sungrazers

The term given to comets that crash into the Sun or get too close to it so that they break up.

NASA's Voyager 1 spacecraft, which launched in 1977, will reach the Oort Cloud in about **300** years.

In 2015 the **SOHO spacecraft** discovered its 3,000th comet. Before it set off in 1995 less than 1,000 comets were known.

The most famous comet is **Halley's Comet**. It comes into the inner solar system and becomes visible about once every 75 to 76 years.

1066 1145 1222 1301 1378 1456 1531 1607 1682 1758 1835 1910 1986 2061

Last came close to Earth in **1986**. Will next be visible in **2061**.

The comet was named after English astronomer **Edmond Halley** (1656–1742). He calculated that a comet seen in 1531, 1607 and 1682 was the same one – and correctly predicted it would be seen again in 1758.

Halley's Comet was first photographed in 1910 when it came within 22.4 million km of Earth.

Halley's Comet features on the historic Bayeux Tapestry, a 70-metre long embroidery created in the 1070s which shows the Battle of Hastings in 1066.

Saturn the ring leader

When you think of Saturn you probably picture its rings, colourful stripes and colossal size. This gas giant has made a massive impact on scientists who have studied its incredible nature for hundreds of years.

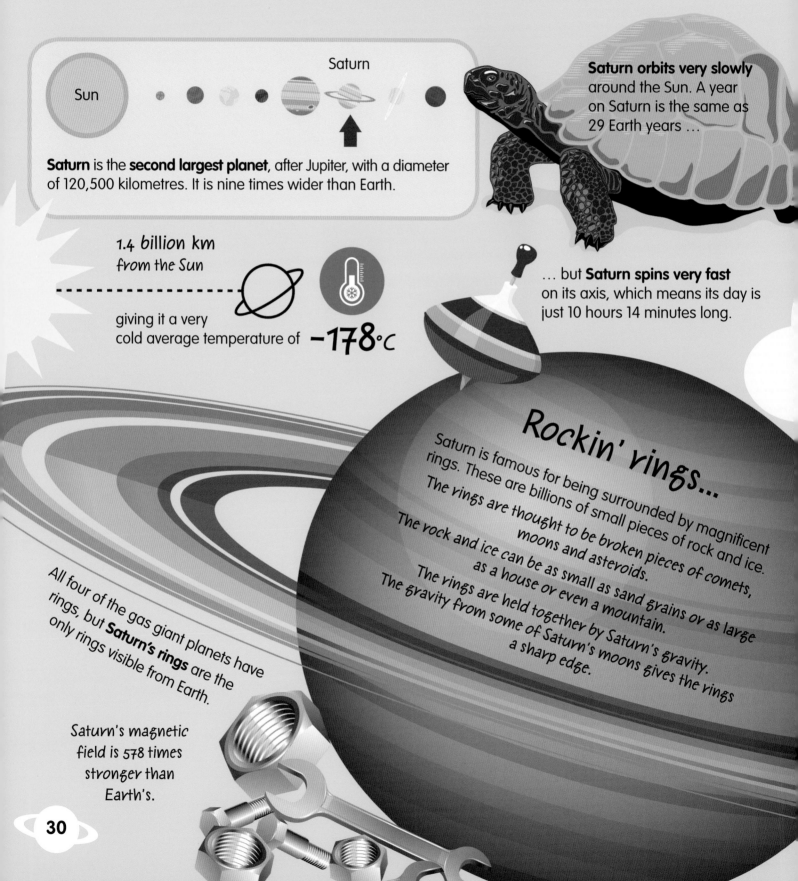

Sun

Saturn

Saturn is the **second largest planet**, after Jupiter, with a diameter of 120,500 kilometres. It is nine times wider than Earth.

Saturn orbits very slowly around the Sun. A year on Saturn is the same as 29 Earth years …

1.4 billion km from the Sun

giving it a very cold average temperature of **−178°C**

… but **Saturn spins very fast** on its axis, which means its day is just 10 hours 14 minutes long.

Rockin' rings...

Saturn is famous for being surrounded by magnificent rings. These are billions of small pieces of rock and ice. The rings are thought to be broken pieces of comets, moons and asteroids. The rock and ice can be as small as sand grains or as large as a house or even a mountain. The rings are held together by Saturn's gravity. The gravity from some of Saturn's moons gives the rings a sharp edge.

All four of the gas giant planets have rings, but **Saturn's rings** are the only rings visible from Earth.

Saturn's magnetic field is 578 times stronger than Earth's.

Even though it's a massive planet, Saturn is not very dense. It's the only planet **less dense than water**.

If you could make a bath big enough, Saturn would float on water!

53

The number of confirmed **moons** that Saturn has, with **9** more waiting to be confirmed.

Saturn's largest moon, Titan, is larger than Earth's Moon.

Above Saturn's north pole is a **hexagonal cloud shape** about 32,000 kilometres wide that reaches 100 kilometres down into Saturn's atmosphere. It has a jet stream raging at 360 kilometres per hour that could have been blowing for hundreds of years.

Saturn is similar to Jupiter, its fellow **gas giant**, because it's made mainly of hydrogen (96.3 per cent) and helium (3.3 per cent).

As with Jupiter, these gases give it a yellowy appearance.

Saturn looks like it has stripes because fierce winds and rising heat create yellow and gold bands.

Saturn can experience **extreme winds**. At its equator these can reach

1,800 km/h

Winds on Earth rarely reach 400 km/h.

7

The number of **main rings** around Saturn. They are all named after letters in the alphabet. A was discovered first and G last.

The largest gap between the rings is between B and A. This is called the **Cassini Division** and is 4,700 kilometres wide.

Between the main rings are darker ringlets and spokes that orbit at different rates to the main rings.

The rings extend 282,000 kilometres from Saturn but …

... each ring is only around 10 metres high on average.

D ring

C ring

B ring

A ring

F ring

G ring

E ring

Spinning sideways with Uranus

Discovered in 1781 by William Herschel, Uranus is an ice giant with a bland surface compared to other planets. There are still lots of incredible facts and stats about it, though.

Sun

Uranus

Uranus is an **ice giant** with no actual surface. The seventh planet from the Sun is made of swirling icy water, methane and ammonia. Only Uranus and Venus rotate in an east to west direction.

97.77 degrees

Uranus has the **largest tilt** of all planets, and looks like it spins on its side. It's believed to be at this strange angle because an object, possibly the size of Earth, collided with it billions of years ago.

90°

It's the **third largest planet**, with a diameter of 51,100 kilometres, which is four times bigger than Earth.

2 1 3

2.9 billion km

from the Sun

2.3% methane and others

15.2% helium

82.5% hydrogen

The methane clouds in Uranus's atmosphere absorb red light, which gives the planet its famous green-blue appearance.

Uranus is a long way from the Sun and is a very cold planet.

−216°C average temperature

Sunlight takes 2 hours 40 minutes to reach Uranus.

More than 19 times further from the Sun than Earth is.

Because Uranus tilts and has a slow orbit around the Sun of 84 Earth years, at times its poles point directly at the Sun.

It has **extreme seasons** with one pole having 21 years of summer sunshine and the other 21 years of winter darkness.

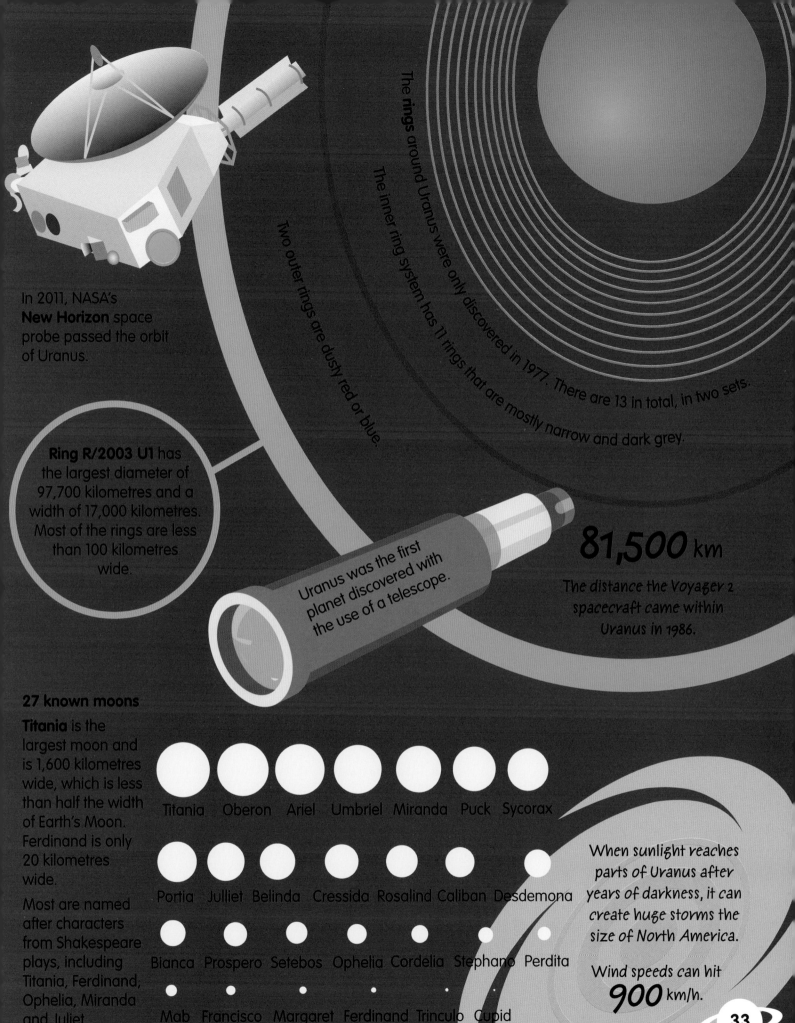

In 2011, NASA's **New Horizon** space probe passed the orbit of Uranus.

The **rings** around Uranus were only discovered in 1977. There are 13 in total, in two sets.

The inner ring system has 11 rings that are mostly narrow and dark grey.

Two outer rings are dusty red or blue.

Ring R/2003 U1 has the largest diameter of 97,700 kilometres and a width of 17,000 kilometres. Most of the rings are less than 100 kilometres wide.

Uranus was the first planet discovered with the use of a telescope.

81,500 km

The distance the Voyager 2 spacecraft came within Uranus in 1986.

27 known moons

Titania is the largest moon and is 1,600 kilometres wide, which is less than half the width of Earth's Moon. Ferdinand is only 20 kilometres wide.

Most are named after characters from Shakespeare plays, including Titania, Ferdinand, Ophelia, Miranda and Juliet.

Titania   Oberon   Ariel   Umbriel   Miranda   Puck   Sycorax

Portia   Julliet   Belinda   Cressida   Rosalind   Caliban   Desdemona

Bianca   Prospero   Setebos   Ophelia   Cordelia   Stephano   Perdita

Mab   Francisco   Margaret   Ferdinand   Trinculo   Cupid

When sunlight reaches parts of Uranus after years of darkness, it can create huge storms the size of North America.

Wind speeds can hit **900** km/h.

On the edge with Neptune

At about 4.5 billion kilometres from Earth and with little sunlight, Neptune is a vast, cold gas planet on the edge of our solar system. Its atmosphere, storms, rings and moons are fascinating to explore.

Fancy coming to my 1st birthday party?

Sun

Neptune

Neptune is the eighth and **furthest planet** from the Sun. It is about 4.5 billion km away, which is over 30 times further than Earth is from the Sun.

165 years
The time it takes Neptune to orbit the Sun.

On Neptune, humans would never have a birthday as we'd live for less than one year!

Like Uranus, Neptune has methane in its atmosphere which makes it blue. But it's a much brighter blue than Uranus so scientists think an unknown component also affects its colouring.

4 × 4

It is four times wider than Earth with a diameter of 49,500 kilometres.

The fourth biggest planet in our solar system.

2011

The year Neptune completed its first orbit since being discovered in 1846.

Neptune is the only planet that can't be seen by the naked eye.

Sunlight takes more than four hours to reach Neptune and is about 900 times dimmer than light on Earth.

04:00

-214°C

Average temperature on Neptune. Astronomers think a heat source inside the planet may stop it being quite as cold as Uranus.

Neptune is the **windiest place** in the solar system. Frozen methane clouds are blasted across it at over 2,000 kilometres an hour, which is faster than the speed of sound.

A fast-moving, bright cloud feature has been nicknamed 'scooter'.

Count me in, Wheeeeee!

Neptune has **13 confirmed moons**. Triton is the largest moon with a diameter of 2,700 kilometres.

I will, if I can shake this darn magnet off.

Neptune's **magnetic field** is 27 times stronger than Earth's.

It is the only large moon in our solar system with a retrograde orbit, which means it spins in the opposition direction to its planet's orbit.

Liberty

Equality

2,700 km — Triton

- Proteus
- Nereid
- Larissa
- Galatea
- Despina
- Thalassa
- Naiad
- Halimede
- Neso
- Sao
- Laomedeia
- Psamathe

There are six known rings around the planet, which were discovered by Voyager 2 in 1989.

Made of dust and rocks

Very dark and difficult to spot

The outer ring, called Adams, is 63,000 kilometres from Neptune. It has three distinctive arcs – called Liberty, Equality and Fraternity.

Fraternity

The **gravity** on Neptune is the closest of all the planets to Earth's gravity. If you stood on Neptune, which you can't because it's a ball of gas, you would only weigh 12 per cent more than you do on Earth.

Unlike Jupiter's, Neptune's storms and weather change quite quickly.

In 1989 Voyager 2 identified a huge dark storm in the south of Neptune that was bigger than Earth. Called **The Great Dark Spot**, it was travelling at 1,200 kilometres per hour – but a few years later it had disappeared.

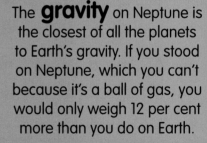

Pluto and the other dwarf planets

Discovered in 1930 and originally called the ninth planet, little Pluto has since been classed as a dwarf planet. And it's not the only dwarf planet. Check out why these distant objects are worth close examination.

Pluto orbits beyond Neptune in a distant zone called the Kuiper Belt. There could be trillions of icy objects in the belt.

5.8 billion km

The average **distance** that Pluto is from the Sun, which is 40 times further from the Sun than Earth is.

Pluto's **diameter** is 2,374 kilometres. It's about two thirds the size of Earth's Moon.

Pluto **orbits in an ellipse shape**, a bit like an oval race track, not in a circle. Because of this, at times it is closer to the Sun. Between 1979 and 1999 Pluto was closer to the Sun than Neptune was.

Pluto can range from about 4.4 billion km to 7.3 billion km away from the Sun.

2006

The year that Pluto was classified a dwarf planet and not one of the eight 'regular' planets in our solar system.

Neptune

Ceres is the only dwarf planet closer to the Sun than Neptune – it is the largest object in the Asteroid Belt.

Diameter of 950 km

Originally called a planet, then an asteroid and finally a dwarf planet.

248 Earth years
The time it takes Pluto to orbit the Sun.

153 Earth hours
How long one day lasts on Pluto.

Transneptunian Objects (TNOs)

The term given to bodies that exist beyond Neptune.

Plutoid

Another name given to a dwarf planet found beyond Neptune.

The first object identified in the Kuiper Belt, in 1992, is called 1992 QB₁.

A dwarf planet must …

 have enough mass and gravity that makes it nearly round

orbit the Sun

A dwarf planet doesn't …

have a path that it has cleared around the Sun, unlike the paths regular planets have. Similar objects to a dwarf planet can cross its path around the Sun.

The three other recognised dwarf planets (so far) are **Eris, Makemake** and **Haumea**.

 Eris was discovered in 2003. It is 2,326 kilometres wide, which is slightly smaller than Pluto.

 Makemake has a reddish colour, perhaps caused by molecules called tholins on the surface.

 Haumea spins on its axis once every four hours and is one of the fastest-spinning large objects in the solar system.

Pluto

There are **5** known moons around Pluto.

Charon

Nix

Hydra

Kerberos

Styx

Styx was discovered in 2012 by the Hubble Space Telescope and is thought to be between 10 and 24 kilometres wide.

-228°C

-238°C

Pluto's surface temperature is extremely cold, ranging from -228°C to -238°C. The coldest recorded temperature on Earth is about -92°C.

Pluto's surface is icy and made up of frozen nitrogen, carbon monoxide and methane.

When Pluto is nearer to the Sun, some of its surface ice changes from solid to a gas and rises to form a thin atmosphere.

What a star!

Look into the sky at night and you can see thousands of tiny bright stars. They may seem small and insignificant, but many are bigger than the Sun and there are billions of stars in the universe.

How a star is born:

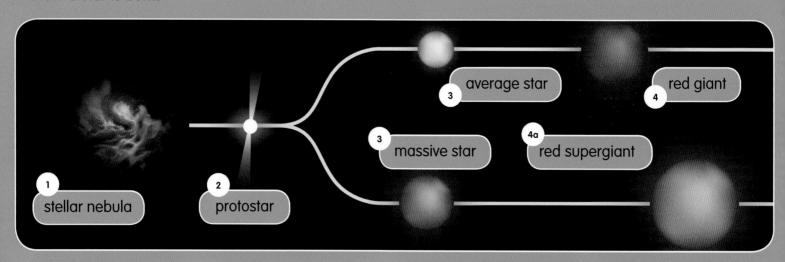

- **1** stellar nebula
- **2** protostar
- **3** average star
- **3** massive star
- **4** red giant
- **4a** red supergiant

1 Huge clouds of gas and dust in space are called **stellar nebulas**. These clouds can be up to 1,500 million kilometres wide.

2 Nebula clouds shrink because of their own gravity and break up into clumps, with each clump forming a young star called a **protostar**.

3 The temperature and density of gas at the protostar's centre causes nuclear reactions, and when it hits 10 million °C it becomes a **true star** with its own heat and light. The star may be average or massive.

3 This process can take around **10 million years** for average stars. Massive stars, which are about 10 times bigger than the Sun, are born much quicker.

Red giants may be up to 150 million km wide.

× **1,700**

the radius of the sun

UY Scuti is the **biggest** known star. Its radius is 1,700 times greater than the Sun.

The **most massive** known star in the universe is called **R136a1**.

250 times the mass of the Sun

8,700,000 times more luminous than the Sun

Stars and their colours and surface temperatures:

2,500 °C   5,500 °C   40,000 °C

Red stars – coolest   Yellow stars – hotter   Blue-white stars – hottest of all

'Failed stars', also known as **brown dwarfs**, are only a few hundred degrees at the surface. They are so cool that their burning nuclear reactions never started.

Stars are not 'star shaped' with pointy ends. They are actually round like the Sun.

That's a lot of baby stars!

Some scientists think that around **275 million new stars** form each day throughout the universe.

How a star dies:

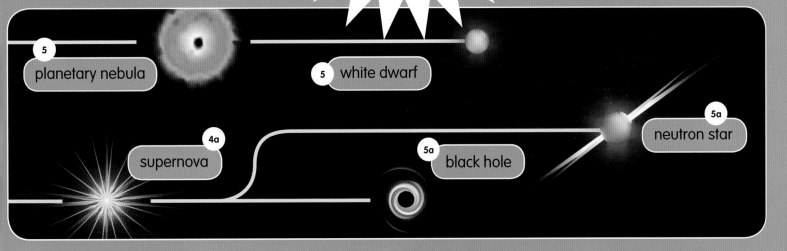

5 planetary nebula

5 white dwarf

5a neutron star

4a supernova

5a black hole

4 When a small star, like the Sun, burns all of its fuel it expands to become a **red giant**.

5 A red giant loses its outer layers, becoming a **planetary nebula**, then cools to become a **white dwarf**.

4a After burning its fuel, a massive star expands to become a **red supergiant** before blowing apart in a **supernova explosion**.

5a The core left over from the explosion produces either a **black hole** or a tiny **neutron star**. Other matter is scattered in space and eventually makes **other stars and planets**.

A constellation is a group of stars in a pattern in the sky.

Columba (dove)

Taurus (bull)

There are 88 official constellations in Earth's sky. Famous constellations include …

Orion (hunter)

Canis Major (big dog)

Constellations can be tricky to spot and most don't look all that much like the object they're named after! But you'll learn with practice!

Twinkle twinkle, little star …

As the light from a star travels through Earth's air the starlight bends and scatters. This makes the star look like it's twinkling.

On average the **Milky Way galaxy**, where our solar system is found, produces about seven new stars each year.

Galaxies near and far

With over 100 billion of them in the universe, galaxies are some of the most fascinating features in space. They form in different shapes and sizes, and large galaxies have mysterious black holes at the centre. Check out these great galactic facts and stats.

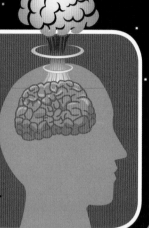

Most stars are part of huge groups called **galaxies**. The Sun, which is the closest star to Earth, is grouped with over 100 billion other stars in a galaxy called the **Milky Way**.

Some scientists think there are more than 125 billion galaxies in the universe.

Galaxies were formed when **groups of stars merged together billions of years ago**. When these galaxies collided their shape and size changed.

220 million years

The time it takes the Sun to circle around the Milky Way's centre.

Black holes

Experts reckon something called a **black hole** is at the centre of most large galaxies. A black hole is a place with phenomenal gravity that sucks anything in that gets too close – even light.

Because black holes pull in light we cannot see them. Special telescopes detect where black holes are.

The Milky Way's supermassive black hole is called Sagittarius A*.

Sagittarius A is as heavy as 4 million Suns.*

Galaxies are grouped in **clusters**. Clusters can range from several galaxies to a few thousand galaxies.

Andromeda
2.5 million light years aw

The Milky Way and Andromeda are part of a cluster called the **Local Group**, which has more than 40 galaxies.

4 main galaxy shapes ...

Elliptical – ball-shaped like a rugby ball. These are the largest galaxies.

Spiral – disc-shaped with a central bulge and spiralling 'arms' with stars on and between them.

Irregular – no regular shape and usually quite small but packed with gas and dust.

Barred spiral – like the spiral but the arms come out from a thick bar-shaped region in the centre.

The Milky Way is in a barred spiral shape.

5 billion years

The time when the Milky Way is predicted to **collide** with its nearest galaxy, Andromeda.

Andromeda is moving towards the Milky Way at about 300 kilometres per second.

Andromeda is the most distant object the human eye can see.

If humans could travel at the speed of light (299,792,458 metres per second) it would still take 2.3 million years to reach Andromeda from the Milky Way.

IC 1101
1 billion light years away

A spiral galaxy called **NGC 7742** *is also known as the* **Fried Egg Galaxy** *because of its bright centre and faint spiral arms.*

The largest known galaxy is an elliptical galaxy called **IC 1101**. It is thought to be nearly 1 billion light years away.

Experts think IC 1101 is between 2 million and 6 million light years in diameter and contains 100 trillion stars.

Perhaps more than 50 Milky Ways could fit across it.

Awesome astronomers

An astronomer is a scientist who studies objects in the sky. Many incredible astronomers have developed our knowledge of the universe over hundreds of years, and here are just some of the most famous and celebrated.

Abd al-Rahman al-Sufi (903–986 CE) lived in what is now Iran and wrote a very famous book called the 'Book of Fixed Stars'. It charted his observations of stars and objects in the sky, including his studies of the Andromeda galaxy.

Johannes Kepler (1571–1630) from Germany built on the studies of Copernicus and came up with laws explaining how planets orbit. They orbit in elliptical shapes, not in circles, they move at different rates in their orbits, and a planet's orbit is determined by its distance from the Sun. Kepler worked closely with Danish astronomer **Tycho Brahe** (1546–1601).

Famous fact!
Although the ancient Greek astronomer **Claudius Ptolemy** (circa 100–170 CE) thought Earth was the centre of the universe, his maps and mathematical methods shaped astronomy for hundreds of years.

Famous fact!
Frenchman **Charles Messier** (1730–1817) recorded around 100 objects that included nebulas, galaxies and star clusters.

Polish astronomer and mathematician **Nicolaus Copernicus** (1473–1543) proposed that Earth and all other planets moved around the Sun. Before this, people thought the Earth was the centre of the solar system. Copernicus' theory, known as the heliocentric ('sun-centred') model, changed our understanding of the universe.

Italian **Galileo Galilei** (1564–1642) developed a powerful telescope and studied the Moon and planets with it. He saw that the Moon was mountainous and cratered, discovered four moons around Jupiter and observed Saturn and the movement of Venus.

Another Italian astronomer, **Giovanni Cassini** (1625–1712) is known for being the first person to observe four of Saturn's moons and for studying Mars and its rotation. He discovered that Saturn's rings have a gap separating them. This gap is now called the Cassini Division.

MIND THE GAP

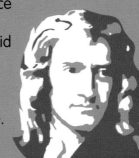

Sir Isaac Newton (1642–1727) was England's most respected astronomer, mathematician and physicist. His work around the laws of motion and gravity has influenced science for over 300 years. Famously, he was said to have developed his theory of gravity after watching an apple fall from a tree.

Famous fact!
18th–19th century German-British astronomer **William Herschel** (1738–1822) discovered Uranus, two moons of Uranus and two moons of Saturn. His sister **Caroline Herschel** (1750–1848) was the first woman to discover a comet.

Famous fact!
British astrophysicist **Jocelyn Bell Burnell** (born 1943) made important discoveries about signals coming from rapidly rotating stars. Her work confirmed the existence of pulsars.

Famous fact!
Christiaan Huygens (1629–1695) developed his own telescope and made detailed observations of Saturn's rings – and spotted its first moon, Titan. The Dutch astronomer made drawings of Mars and came up with a wave theory of light.

German **Albert Einstein** (1879–1955) revolutionised our understanding of the universe. His 'special theory of relativity' states that the laws of physics are the same throughout the universe. His 'general relativity' theory says space and time are linked, and are distorted by massive objects' gravity.

American **Henrietta Swan Leavitt** (1868–1921) developed our understanding of how stars brighten and dim, meaning the distance of stars and galaxies could later be calculated.

Famous fact!
American **William Hartmann** (born 1939) is credited with explaining how the Moon was formed after a collision with Earth.

Studying space from Earth

People have looked up into the skies and out into the universe for thousands of years. And for over 400 years, telescopes – which use lenses or mirrors to magnify faraway objects – have helped us see clearer and further.

Over **3,000 years ago**, **astronomers** were already monitoring the movements of stars and planets.

This helped keep track of time, which in turn helped with things like when to farm land and when to perform religious ceremonies.

Stonehenge, England, is one of many structures we think were used by ancient astronomers.

1000 CE (approximately)
The time of the **first recorded astronomical observations**, from ancient Mesopotamia (modern-day Iraq).

300 CE onwards
Ancient Greek astronomers, such as Aristarchus of Samos, began to predict how far away objects in the sky really were and the relative size of the Sun, Moon and Earth.

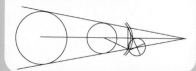

15th century
Ulugh Beg, an astronomer, mathematician and ruler of a large part of central Asia, built a big **sextant** with a radius of 36 metres so he could study the sky. He recorded 994 stars.

A sextant is a device for measuring the angular distance between two objects.

200 CE onwards
Hipparchus of Nicaea recorded the position of 850 **stars** using just his eyes and basic instruments like this **astrolabe**.

The **first telescope** originated from Holland around **1608**. **Hans Lippershay** (sometimes written as Lipperhey) is often credited as inventing it, but others argued that they were the first.

In **1609**, Italian **Galileo Galilei** (page 42) was the first to use a telescope to study the sky.

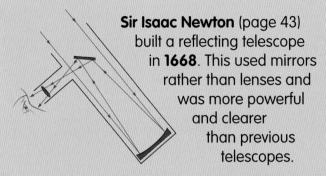

Sir Isaac Newton (page 43) built a reflecting telescope in **1668**. This used mirrors rather than lenses and was more powerful and clearer than previous telescopes.

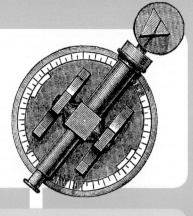

In the early **1800s**, an instrument called a **spectroscope** allowed astronomers to study what objects were made of and how they moved.

NASA's 10-metre wide **Keck I** and **Keck II** telescopes, in Hawaii, USA, first detected the dwarf planet Eris in **2005**. This led to astronomers inventing a whole new category of objects – dwarf planets – and to Pluto being reclassified as a dwarf planet.

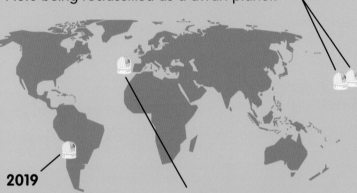

2019 is the year that the **Large Synoptic Survey Telescope (LSST)** will begin surveying the universe from its base in Chile.

The European Space Agency's **Teide Observatory** in Tenerife, Spain, detects potentially dangerous human-made debris, or '**space junk**', orbiting as high as 36,000 kilometres above Earth.

Extremely Large Telescope

This huge telescope, based in Chile, is due to begin studying the sky in **2024**.

39-metre wide reflecting mirror – the largest in the world

Overall structure about the size of the London Eye, London, UK

LSST facts

3,200 megapixel camera

10-year operation to image the universe

Estimated camera cost $165 million, total project cost over $400 million.

Space objects you can spot using just your eyes:

The **International Space Station** is usually the brightest object after the Moon. It moves fast and doesn't twinkle. Visit spotthestation.nasa.gov to find out when to see it where you are.

The **Moon** is always fascinating to watch and study, especially on a clear night when there's a full Moon – every 29.5 days.

A **meteor shower** is best seen without a telescope or binoculars. Using just your eyes you'll see a wider range of the sky … and increase your chances of spotting one!

FAST fact

Radio telescopes detect radio waves, rather than light, from space objects.

In 2016 the giant **F**ive-hundred-metre **A**perture **S**pherical **T**elescope (**FAST**) was completed in China.

500 metres wide and the world's largest solid single dish radio telescope.

The dish antenna has 4,450 individual panels.

Amazing astronauts

Being an astronaut really is an 'out of this world' job! It takes special skills and years of training to become one. Orbiting Earth, performing spacewalks and walking on the Moon are some of the incredible achievements astronauts have made.

The **first person in space** was the Soviet Union's (now Russia's) **Yuri Gagarin** in 1961. The Soviets used the word 'cosmonaut' instead of astronaut, but it means the same thing.

Gagarin was 27 when he set the record. He only went to space once. He was tragically killed in a plane crash in 1968.

An astronaut's spacesuit is white because white reflects heat. The temperature in space in direct sunlight can reach over 130°C.

5 days

In 1963 cosmonaut **Valery Bykovsky** spent five days by himself in Earth's orbit on *Vostok 5*. It's still the longest solo space mission.

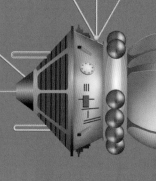

879 days

The most time, in total, spent in space by an astronaut or cosmonaut. Russia's **Gennady Padalka** set the record in 2015.

Soviet cosmonaut **Valentina Tereshkova** became the first woman in space in June 1963. Her mission on the *Vostok 6* spacecraft lasted two days, 23 hours and 12 minutes.

1983

The year that **Sally Ride** became the first female American astronaut in space, on board the *Challenger* space shuttle.

Extravehicular activity (EVA) is the technical term for a spacewalk, when astronauts or cosmonauts leave their spacecraft in space.

The Soviet Union's *Alexei Leonov* carried out the first spacewalk in March 1965 – it lasted 12 minutes.

Spacesuits have several layers and materials. The arms have 14 layers, including a bullet-proof layer as protection against flying objects in space.

1. Liquid Cooling and Ventilation Garment (LCVG) Liner

2. LCVG Liner Outer Layer

3. LCVG Liner Water Transport Tubing

4. Pressure Garment Bladder

5. Restraint

6. Thermal Micrometeroid Garment (TMG) Layer

7–13. TMG Liner

14. TMG Cover

In 1984, NASA's **Bruce McCandless** made the first spacewalk without being attached to a spacecraft. Using a nitrogen jet-propelled backpack, Bruce travelled about 100 metres from the *Challenger* orbiter.

In 2015 **Tim Peake** became the first British astronaut to reach the ISS. His mission lasted 186 days, covered about 125 million kilometres and saw 2,976 orbits of Earth.

The NASA astronaut who has spent the most time in space is **Peggy Whitson**. After returning to Earth from the ISS in September 2017, she had clocked up **665** days in space during three separate missions.

Peggy has made 10 spacewalks, lasting 60 hours and 21 minutes.

Inside the ISS, astronauts can operate a human-like robot called **Robonaut 2**. The clever robot can be programmed to perform tasks and help astronauts with experiments.

Robonaut 2 cost about $17 million.

12 NASA astronauts who walked on the Moon . . . .

1 Neil Armstrong (July 1969)

2 Buzz Aldrin (July 1969)

3 Pete Conrad (Nov 1969)

4 Alan Bean (Nov 1969)

5 Alan Shepard (Feb 1971)

6 Edgar Mitchell (Feb 1971)

7 David Scott (Aug 1971)

8 James Irwin (Aug 1971)

9 John Young (Apr 1972)

10 Charles Duke (Apr 1972)

11 Eugene Cernan (Dec 1972)

12 Harrison Schmitt (Dec 1972)

International Space Station

The International Space Station (ISS) took 13 years to construct. Probably the most incredible machine ever made, it was built in space, at a cost of around $100 billion. Its main role is for astronauts to conduct science experiments in low Earth orbit.

The **ISS travels** at about 400 kilometres above Earth at an average speed of 27,700 kilometres an hour, which is 7.7 kilometres every second.

It orbits Earth 16 times each day, circling the planet every 90 minutes.

Through the NASA website you can have text alerts sent to your phone telling you when the ISS is flying over your area.

After the Moon, the ISS is the **brightest object in the night sky**. It's best viewed at night-time.

The **eight huge solar arrays** (solar panels) on the ISS each have a wingspan of 73 metres. They contain 262,400 solar cells that use sunlight to power the spacecraft.

The solar arrays produce enough **electricity** to power 40 homes.

52 computers control the complex systems on the ISS. × 52

Over **12 km of wiring** connects the electrical power system. 12 km

The **robotic arm** on the outside of the ISS can lift nearly 100,000 kg.

100,000 kg

Up to **six astronauts** can live on the ISS at one time. An astronaut usually stays for several months at a time.

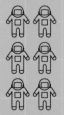

The ISS has been continually occupied since **November 2000**.

Between December 1998 and September 2017, **202 spacewalks** have happened.

Spacewalks can last between one and nine hours.

During spacewalks astronauts can do experiments, test equipment or make repairs.

The Russian **Soyuz capsule** can transport three astronauts to the ISS in about six hours, although if there are problems it can take up to two days.

There are many different foods for the astronauts to eat on the ISS, including chicken, beef, nuts, fruit, chocolate and seafood.

Salt and pepper is only available in liquid form. Salt and pepper grains would float away.

Each astronaut spends about **35** hours a week conducting experiments on the ISS.

There are **3** laboratories.

Over **150** experiments take place at once.

Astronauts on the ISS do not feel the effect of Earth's gravity so much, so it takes less use of their muscles to do ordinary things. To stay strong they have to **exercise** for about two hours each day. This includes running on a treadmill and cycling on a fixed bike.

In total, 15 countries, including the USA, Russia, Canada, Japan, Germany, Sweden and Netherlands, worked together to construct the ISS.

There is a shower unit on the ISS, but astronauts don't like to use it as water droplets float around in space! Most astronauts use a flannel or wipes to wash, using soap that doesn't need rinsing.

The ISS weighs 419,725 kg and is 109 m long.

It has 18 major parts.

More than 115 spaceflights were needed to build it.

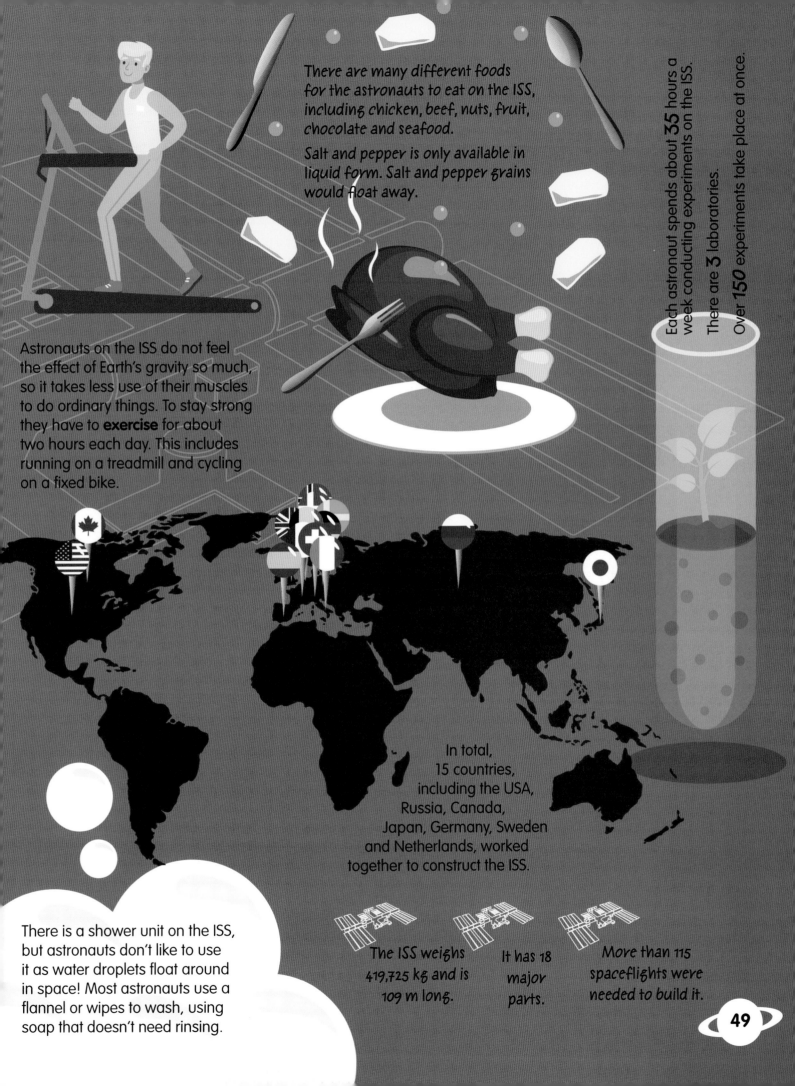

Super spacecraft

From flying telescopes to probes, rovers and space shuttles, spacecraft are amazingly complex machines. Here you can uncover all sorts of spectacular facts about these 'out of this world' creations.

Hubble is a NASA telescope orbiting Earth at about 547 kilometres above the surface. It was launched in 1990 by the *Discovery* space shuttle. Unlike the ISS no humans are on Hubble apart from when it's repaired.

 13.3 metres long and over 12,000 kg

 Travels more than 27,000 km/h

 95 minutes to orbit Earth

 Hubble detects objects 10 billion times fainter than the human eye can see

 Has made more than 1.3 million observations.

In 2016 Hubble measured an infant galaxy, called **GN-z11**, as it was seen 13.4 billion years ago. It's the farthest galaxy ever viewed.

In 1981 NASA's **Space Shuttle** became the first reusable spacecraft to carry humans into orbit.

5 space shuttles used 1981–2011
Reach speed of about 28,000 km/h
Missions cost $113.7 billion
864,401,219 km flown
20,952 Earth orbits

Hubble studies the universe in **infrared, visible** and **ultraviolet light**.

Radio 10^3 Microwave 10^{-2} Infrared 10^{-5} Visible 0.5×10^{-6} Ultraviolet 10^{-8} X-ray 10^{-10} Gamma ray 10^{-12}

Wavelength (m)

Frequency (Hz)

It's named after American **astronomer Edwin Hubble** (1889–1953), who observed the existence of galaxies beyond the Milky Way and helped show that the universe is expanding.

Three Lunar Roving Vehicles (LRVs) were driven on the Moon by NASA *Apollo* mission astronauts in the 1970s. They were nicknamed moon buggies.

210 kg
Driven **90** km in total
First LRV cost **$38** million
(equivalent of about $228 million in 2017)

Since 1995 the spacecraft **SOHO** (Solar and Heliospheric Observatory) has been studying the Sun and solar wind. It can see about

20 million kilometres beyond the Sun.

SOHO cost about €1 billion. It has also discovered more than 3,000 comets.

URO

At last! I've got a pile of washing the size of Jupiter!

In 2014 the European Space Agency's *Rosetta* spacecraft became the first to land on a comet. After travelling for 10 years *Rosetta* sent a small lander, called Philae, onto the surface of comet Churyumov-Gerasimenko (which is about 4.3 km long).

Philae was only about the size of a washing machine.

The USA's **Viking 1** became the first spacecraft to land on Mars – on 20 July 1976 – and successfully complete its mission.

The Soviet spacecraft *Venera 7* landed on the surface of Venus in 1970. It was the first machine to land on another planet and successfully transmit data back to Earth.

A robotic rover called **Opportunity** has been exploring Mars since January 2004. It moves slowly on the 'red planet' and by September 2017 had covered 45 kilometres on the surface.

Opportunity takes images, examines rocks and even drills the surface of Mars.

Voyager 1 has travelled the greatest distance of any spacecraft. Launched in 1977, by October 2017 the NASA probe was more than 21 billion kilometres from Earth – and still voyaging.

The twin **Voyager 2** was launched 16 days before *Voyager 1* and by October 2017 it was over 17 billion kilometres away from our planet.

The **first spacecraft to land on the Moon** was an unmanned Soviet Union probe called **Luna 2**. It was deliberately crashed into the Moon's surface in September 1959 so scientists could study the impact it made on the ground and in the atmosphere.

Voyager 1 travels at an estimated speed of more than

61,000 km/h

That's pretty fast!

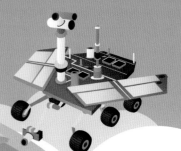

Space around the world

NASA's and Russia's achievements in space technology are well known, but did you know that countries like China, Canada and several European countries have made their mark in space exploration too?

NASA (National Aeronautics and Space Administration) is the USA's space agency and the most famous space organisation in the world. It was set up in 1958, when it employed about 8,000 people with an annual budget of $100 million.

In 2018, NASA's annual budget was

$19.1 billion

NASA's **Space Shuttle** missions (1981–2011) used the iconic Space Shuttle spacecraft.

852 crew flew on 135 Space Shuttle missions.

44

305

In October 2017, NASA had 44 active astronauts.

Another 305 astronauts have worked with NASA since 1958.

NASA's *Apollo* missions, with manned flights between 1967 and 1972, were famous for putting humans on the Moon. *Apollo 11*, in July 1969, took Neil Armstrong and Buzz Aldrin to the surface.

2 planned NASA missions …

Mars 2020 – robotic rover to explore Mars for two years, landing in February 2021.

Proposed for 2023 – Fast Infrared Exoplanet Spectroscopy Survey Explorer (FINESSE) will survey over 500 planets beyond our solar system.

One of the CSA's most important creations is Canadarm, a 15-metre long robotic arm which was first used on NASA's Space Shuttle program.

In space Canadarm could lift over **265,000 kg.**

NASA's **first human flight mission** was called *Mercury,* with six flights between 1961 and 1963.

The **Canadian Space Agency** (CSA) was formed in 1989.

14

14 Canadians have been astronauts.

Canadarm 2 was taken to the ISS in 2001.

Canadarm 2

17.6 m long

The European Space Agency (ESA) was set up in 1975.

Over 2,000 people work for the ESA.

Headquarters are in Paris, France

ESA helps conduct lots of experiments on the ISS, builds and maintains satellites, monitors the solar system from Earth and trains astronauts.

The **UK Space Agency** contributes £9.1 billion each year to the UK economy and creates 28,900 jobs.

2 planned ESA missions ...

Advanced Telescope for High-Energy Astrophysics (ATHENA), to launch in 2028, will map hot gas structures and search for supermassive black holes.

The Earth Cloud Aerosol and Radiation Explorer (EarthCARE) satellite will study clouds and aerosols and how they trap or reflect the Sun's light.

ROSCOSMOS
ESA
UK SPACE AGENCY
CANADIAN SPACE AGENCY
NASA
CHINESE NATIONAL SPACE ADMINISTRATION

Russia's space agency is **ROSCOSMOS**, set up in 2015. Before that it was the Russian Space Agency and before that the Soviet space program.

ROSCOSMOS's main launch base is in Baikonur, Kazakhstan, with nine launch sites. A new space centre, the Vostochny Cosmodrome, is due to be completed in 2018.

The space centre covers
700 sq km.

By 2020 45 per cent of Russia's spacecraft will be launched from Vostochny.

Vostochny Cosmodrome

Between 2019 and 2022 the **China National Space Administration** plans to build its own space station.

22 countries are part of the ESA ...

Austria
Belgium
Czech Republic
Denmark
Estonia
Finland
France
Germany
Greece
Hungary
Ireland
Italy
Luxembourg
Netherlands
Norway
Poland
Portugal
Romania
Spain
Sweden
Switzerland
United Kingdom

The Space Race

For an exciting few decades of the 20th century, the USA and the Soviet Union (now Russia) battled to become the most successful nation in spaceflight and space technology. This battle was called the Space Race.

1945

When the Second World War ends, many of Germany's rocket engineers, including Wernher von Braun who helped create the V-2 rocket used during the war, move to the US to develop America's early space technology.

1955

In 1955 both the US and Soviet Union say they are preparing to send objects into space within a few years. These statements mark the beginning of the Space Race.

1957

On 4 October 1957, the Soviet Union's small Sputnik 1 satellite becomes the first human-made object to orbit Earth. Launched by rocket, it is 58 centimetres wide and orbits Earth in around 98 minutes. In about three months Sputnik 1 completes approximately 1,400 orbits and travels 70 million kilometres.

1957

In November Sputnik 2 orbits Earth carrying a dog called Laika, who becomes the first animal to orbit the Earth. Sadly Laika dies during the flight.

1957

On 6 December, the USA's *Vanguard* rocket explodes seconds after launch as the country fails to send its first object into orbit.

1958

On 31 January the US successfully sends a spacecraft into orbit. The Explorer 1 satellite makes important discoveries about radiation in Earth's orbit.

1959

In April 1959 NASA unveils its first group of seven astronauts, known as the Mercury Seven. The US hopes the astronauts will soon be carrying out missions in space.

1959

In August NASA's Explorer 6 satellite takes the first photograph of Earth from space.

1959

The Soviet Union's *Luna 2* spacecraft becomes the first object to reach the Moon when it is deliberately crashed into the surface in September 1959.

1961

In a huge victory for the Soviet Union, Yuri Gagarin becomes the first human in space on April 12 1961, aboard *Vostok 1*. He spends 108 minutes orbiting Earth.

1961

Just a few weeks after Gagarin, Alan Shepard wins the honour of being the first American in space. His flight aboard the rocket *Mercury Freedom 7* lasts less than 15 minutes.

15 minutes

1961

US President John F. Kennedy announces that before the end of the sixties an American will land on the Moon and return safely.

1962

NASA's Mariner 2 is the first spacecraft to perform a 'flyby' of another planet. It comes within 34,000 kilometres of Venus and sends data back to Earth.

1963

The Soviet Union's Valentina Tereshkova becomes the first woman to fly into space.

1965

In March 1965 Russian cosmonaut Alexei Leonov is the first person to perform a spacewalk. He reaches space on a rocket called *Voskhod 2* and spends 12 minutes outside his spacecraft.

1966

The Russian probe Luna 10 is the first spacecraft to orbit the Moon. No astronauts are on board.

1968

In December 1968, three American astronauts become the first to orbit the Moon. Jim Lovell, William Anders and Frank Borman are on *Apollo 8*, powered by a *Saturn V* rocket.

1969

The biggest moment in the space race is on 20 July 1969, when NASA astronauts Neil Armstrong and Buzz Aldrin walk on the Moon. Their Apollo 11 mission is the first time humans have touched the Moon's surface.

1971

The Soviet Union creates the first space station, Salyut 1. Sadly, cosmonauts Georgi Dobrovolksi, Vladislav Vokov and Viktor Patsayev died on their journey back to Earth.

1972

In December 1972 Apollo 17 is the last of NASA's six Moon landing missions. The USA is the only nation that has sent astronauts to the Moon.

1975

The *Apollo-Soyuz* mission in 1975 sees American and Russian spacecraft docked together in space, with their astronauts spending several hours together. This cooperation instead of competition is widely seen as the end of the Space Race.

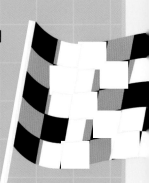

Space spin-offs

Space technology powers spacecraft and lets humans explore the solar system, but it also has many benefits in everyday life on Earth. This is known as a 'spin-off' from the space industry.

The design and technology of the Apollo astronaut spacesuits helped make **trainers** more comfortable.

The process used to make the spacesuit helmet, called blow rubber moulding, was applied to create hollow shoe soles that could be filled with shock-absorbing materials.

Frank Rudy, a former NASA engineer, helped create the famous Nike Air cushioned trainer.

The Reliant Stadium in Houston, Texas, USA, was the first to have a **retractable roof** that could slide away. The roof's material was based on the fabric used in NASA spacesuits. The material …

is lightweight

is stronger than steel

allows a good level of light through.

The development of **battery-powered drills** is thanks to space missions. NASA asked the American company Black & Decker to design a small, lightweight drill that could be used by astronauts on the Moon to drill rocks.

In the early 1970s a **firefighter's breathing apparatus** was heavy, weighing over 13 kilograms. After four years of testing, NASA built a system that weighed one third less and allowed a firefighter to see better in smoke and darkness.

Black & Decker's technology led to battery drills becoming popular on Earth.

Handheld vacuum cleaners, known as 'dust busters', are also a result of NASA work.

The use of **solar panels** on Earth is possible because of NASA technology used in the Apollo Moon landing missions.

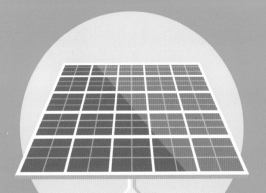

At the **2008 Olympics**, 94 per cent of gold-medal winning swimmers wore a new swimsuit developed at a NASA research centre. The suit was designed to be streamlined and fast in the water.

Light-emitting diode (LED) devices used to help grow plants on the International Space Station have also helped to heal human wounds and relieve pain.

More Earth-based technology developed from NASA work ...

Heart monitors

Air-powered lifting machines

Intruder alarms

Swimming pool water purifiers

Earthquake testing and monitoring equipment.

Since 1976 more than 1,600 NASA technologies have been used by American businesses.

Using technology designed to let ISS astronauts conduct experiments just from a laptop computer, a company developed a clever Earth-based oven. The oven keeps food chilled and then automatically cooks it at a set time. The oven can be controlled using a mobile phone or Internet connection.

0:15

PING! Message received.

A special alloy material used on the ISS was developed for use in some golf clubs.

Golf ball designs have also been influenced by using NASA's high-speed video technology and the technology used to test the Space Shuttle's fuel tank.

Looking for life

Scientists are eager to know if any form of life exists, or ever did exist, away from Earth. Some planets and moons show evidence of this, and we are still searching for life beyond our home ....

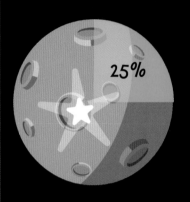

25%

In 2013 a distant planet outside our solar system was detected and picked as a place where life could possibly be supported. Called **HD 40307g**, the planet is about 90 million kilometres from its star, which means it may be hot enough to have Earth-like conditions.

Enceladus is Saturn's sixth largest moon. Might life exist there?

Hi, I'm Earth

Nice to meet you. I'm HD 40307g.

Scientists think the **dwarf planet Ceres**, the largest object in the Asteroid Belt, could be made up of 25 per cent water. This would mean it has more water than Earth. If there is water below the surface of Ceres, it could mean life is there now or was in the past.

NASA's Dawn orbiter has orbited Ceres, looking for signs of life. It took over seven years to get there.

In 2005 NASA's Cassini spacecraft discovered water vapour gushing from Enceladus's surface.

The gushes could come from an underground ocean.

If Enceladus has an ocean, it could be home to life forms.

Voyager 1 and **Voyager 2**, launched in 1977 and currently travelling more than 17 billion kilometres from Earth, each carry a special time capsule called the Golden Record.

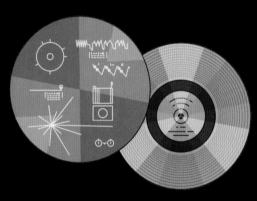

It's designed to show what life on Earth is like if found by another life form.

Saturn's moon Titan could have a salty ocean that begins between 50 and 100 kilometres below its surface.

In the future, NASA experts could explore Titan using robotic boats, balloons or submarines.

The Hubble Space Telescope has detected similar watery plumes to Enceladus's coming from Jupiter's moon Europa.

Below its surface, Europa could have two or three times more water than there is in Earth's oceans.

Has 115 images of things like humans, animals, buildings and solar system planets

Contains spoken human messages in 55 languages

Has sound recordings of animals, waves, wind and thunder

Has 90 minutes of music.

The **Search for Extraterrestrial Intelligence (SETI)** Institute was set up in 1984 and helps to organise this work. So far no extraterrestrial signals have been detected.

Many **telescopes and satellites** on Earth search for signals that suggest non-human life may exist in the universe.

3 reasons why humans would struggle to live on Mars …

Extreme cold

Fierce winds

No oxygen in the atmosphere

Also, it would take approximately nine months to reach Mars.

Approximately **124 meteorites** found on Earth are identified as having come from Mars.

✹ **NASA's Curiosity rover** landed on Mars in 2012 and is searching for evidence that the planet once supported small life forms called microbes.

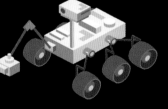

In the 2030s NASA hopes to be able to send humans into orbit around Mars.

The most famous Mars meteorite, ALH 84001, was found in Antarctica in 1984. Tiny carbonate grains in the meteorite suggest it was once immersed in water on Mars.

✹ 17 cameras to take images of the surface

✹ Laser that can vaporise small rocks

✹ 2-metre long arm to move tools.

Weird, wacky and wonderful

Space is packed with 'out of this world' information, but these facts and stats could blow your mind! Read on to unearth a stack of weird, wonderful and wacky things.

In 2017 astronauts on the International Space Station played with a **fidget spinner**. They spun the toy, then let go and watched it float and spin in microgravity.

The Olympic torch has been into space with astronauts three times, in 1996, 2000 and 2014. It went on a spacewalk in 2014.

The torch's flame wasn't lit when it was in space.

Three **LEGO** minifigures are onboard the Juno spacecraft, which reached Jupiter's orbit in 2016 after five years of travelling. The 4-centimetre-high figures are of the Roman gods Juno and Jupiter and astronomer Galileo Galilei.

The god Pluto

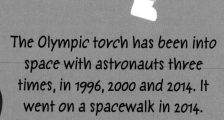

William Herschel, who **discovered Uranus** in 1781, originally tried to call it Georgium Sidus, which means the Georgian Planet, in honour of King George III.

The fastest pieces of **space debris** can reach 50,000 kilometres per hour, which is 17 times faster than a bullet from a machine gun!

In 1930 an 11-year-old English girl called Venetia Burney suggested naming a newly-discovered planet **Pluto**. Her grandfather sent the idea to an observatory in the USA, and soon the planet (now dwarf planet) got its name.

British astronaut Tim Peake ran 42 kilometres, the length of a marathon, on a treadmill while on the ISS in 2016. Tim was the second person to 'run a marathon' in space, after Sunita Williams in 2007. Tim ran a record time of:

3 HRS 35 MINS 21 SECS

In 1947 the USA sent **fruit flies into space** on a V-2 rocket. They flew over 100 kilometres above the surface, and returned to Earth safely. They were the first animals to enter space.

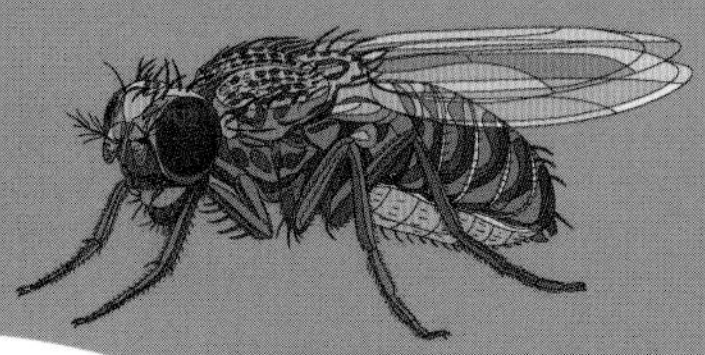

That's a good name for an astronaut.

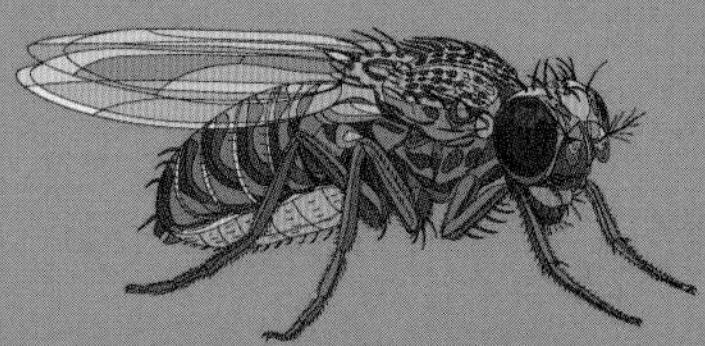

Buzz...

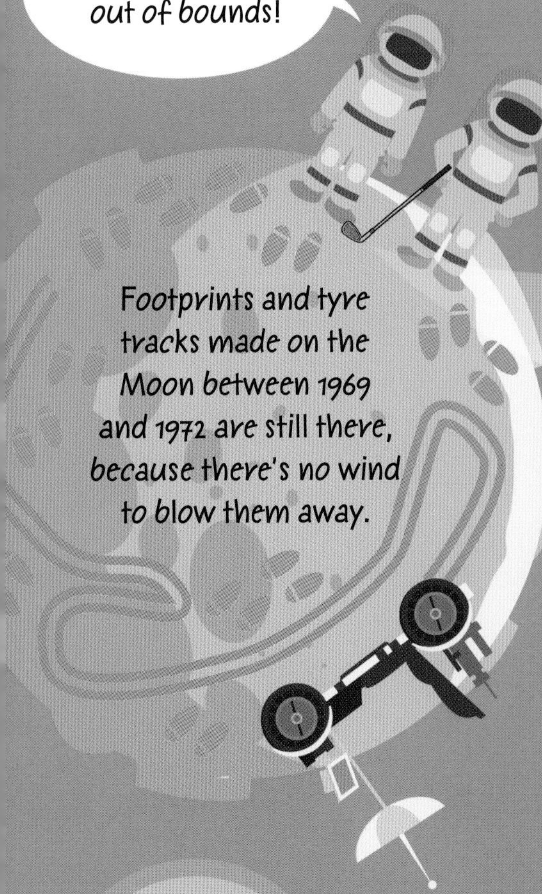

That's definitely out of bounds!

In 1971, astronaut Alan Shepard hit a golf ball on the Moon. Some experts reckon the ball would have travelled for more than 1.5 kilometres because of the low gravity there.

Footprints and tyre tracks made on the Moon between 1969 and 1972 are still there, because there's no wind to blow them away.

For every six months an astronaut spends in space, he or she ages less than humans on Earth by about 0.007 seconds. This is because the speed that time passes changes when travelling very fast.

437 days

Russia's Valeri Polyakov spent a record **437 consecutive days in space** between 1994 and 1995, ageing 0.017 seconds less than people on Earth during this time.

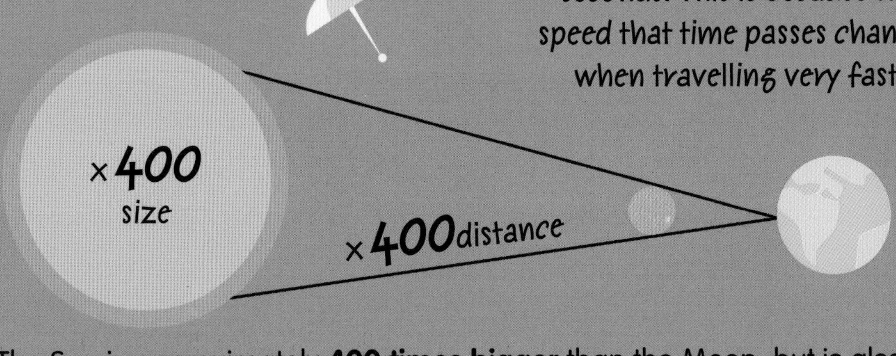

×**400** size

×**400** distance

The Sun is approximately **400 times bigger** than the Moon, but is also about **400 times further away** from Earth than the Moon is. This means that, when viewed from Earth, both appear to be about the same size.

61

Space: more things to find

This book is packed with 'out of this world' facts, stats, numbers and guides, but there's so much more for you to discover in spectacular space! Here's a helpful list of interesting and exciting websites that will expand your knowledge of the planets, space travel and exploration.

International Space Station

Official NASA International Space Station: www.nasa.gov/mission_pages/station

Spot The Station: spotthestation.nasa.gov

Mobile or email sighting alerts: spotthestation.nasa.gov/signup.cfm

Tours: www.nasa.gov/mission_pages/station/main/suni_iss_tour.html

Tracker: www.esa.int/Our_Activities/Human_Spaceflight/International_Space_Station and click 'Where is the International Space Station?'

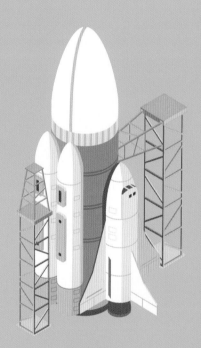

NASA

Home page: www.nasa.gov

NASA TV: www.nasa.gov/multimedia/nasatv

Journey to Mars: www.nasa.gov/content/nasas-journey-to-mars

Mars Spirit and Opportunity: www.nasa.gov/mission_pages/mer/index.html

Image of the Day: www.nasa.gov/multimedia/imagegallery/iotd.html

History: www.nasa.gov/topics/history/index.html

YouTube: www.youtube.com/user/NASAtelevision/videos

Podcasts: www.nasa.gov/podcasts

European Space Agency

Home page: www.esa.int/ESA

Astronauts: www.esa.int/Our_Activities/Human_and_Robotic_Exploration/Astronauts

European Astronaut Centre: www.esa.int/About_Us/EAC

Observing Earth: www.esa.int/Our_Activities/Observing_the_Earth

Videos: www.esa.int/spacevideos/videos

ESA for Kids: www.esa.int/kids/en/home

News: www.esa.int/Our_Activities/Space_News

Astronomy

The Royal Astronomical Society: https://ras.ac.uk/

British Astronomical Association: https://britastro.org/

American Astronomical Society: https://aas.org

NASA Amateur Astronomy: www.nasa.gov/vision/universe/watchtheskies/stars_hobby.html

International Meteor Organization: www.imo.net

The Planetary Society: www.planetary.org

Attractions
NASA Visitor Centres: www.visitnasa.com
ESA guided tours: www.esa.int/About_Us/ESOC/ESOC_guided_tours
Euro Space Center: www.eurospacecenter.be/en
Royal Observatory Greenwich: www.rmg.co.uk/royal-observatory
UK National Space Centre: https://spacecentre.co.uk
Museum of Cosmonautics: www.kosmo-museum.ru

Telescopes
Hubble Space Telescope: www.nasa.gov/mission_pages/hubble/main/index.html and sci.esa.int/hubble
James Webb Space Telescope: www.jwst.nasa.gov
Keck Observatory: www.keckobservatory.org/media/cosmic-cams/
European Southern Observatory: www.eso.org

General
Google Earth: https://earth.google.com/web
NASA news: www.jpl.nasa.gov/news
Live view from ISS: www.ustream.tv/channel/live-iss-stream
Solar system guide: https://solarsystem.nasa.gov/planets

Stories of astronomers, astronauts and other space scientists
Apollo 13 (film telling the story of this spacecraft's dramatic brush with disaster, 1995)
Dogs in Space: the Amazing True Story of Belka and Strelka by Vix Southgate and Iris Deppe (Wren and Rook, 2018)
   – book telling the story of two dogs that went to space and came back safely
For All Mankind (documentary film featuring all 24 men who have been to the Moon, 1989)
Ground Control to Major Tim by Clive Gifford (Wayland, 2017)
   – book about British astronaut Tim Peake's early life and adventures in space
Galileo Galilei (Scientists Who Made History) by Mike Goldsmith (Wayland, 2014)
   – book about the pioneer of astronomy
Hidden Figures (film telling the story of the African-American women whose work
     helped launch men into space, 2016)

Index

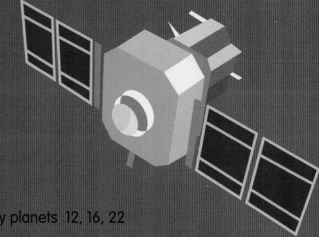